From the huge cloud of jewels that was his life
Fell a torrential rain of dharma deep and vast.
It soaked the dry soil of beings' hearts.
I will share this ambrosial garland of his secret vajra speech.

Treasury of Eloquence

The Songs of Barway Dorje

Translated by Yeshe Gyamtso

KTD Publications
Woodstock, New York

Published by KTD Publications
335 Meads Mountain Road
Woodstock, NY 12498, USA
www.KTDPublications.org

Distributed by Namse Bangdzo Bookstore
www.NamseBangdzo.com

Thangka of Barway Dorje: painted by Terchen Barway Dorje,
photographed by Bardor Tulku Rinpoche (front cover, pages vi, 4)
Clouds by Huang Hanping
Photograph of Bardor Tulku Rinpoche by Basia Coulter

Printed in the USA

ISBN: 978-1-934608-00-5
This book is printed on acid-free paper

Contents

This detail from the thangka shown on the cover depicts Terchen Barway Dorje with Vajrasattva above him. It was painted by Barway Dorje and is kept at Raktrul Monastery in East Tibet. Photograph by Bardor Tulku Rinpoche.

Translator's Introduction

The realization songs composed by great Buddhist teachers of India and Tibet are a tremendous source of both instruction and inspiration for all Buddhists and all who practice meditation. *Treasury of Eloquence* is a collection of songs and instructions composed by the great treasure-revealer and visionary teacher Barway Dorje (1836-1918), whose biography, *Precious Essence*, has also been translated and published. *Treasury of Eloquence* also includes several songs and poems written by some of Barway Dorje's disciples, including the compiler of this collection, Kagyu Tashi of Kyodrak Monastery.

In compiling this collection, Kagyu Tashi added only its title; a brief introduction, consisting of two stanzas of verse and four sentences of prose; and some of the prefaces and colophons that accompany the individual songs.

Included in this collection are songs expressing Barway Dorje's devotion to his gurus, songs explaining how to meditate on the mind's nature, and songs of advice on the practice of Buddhism in general.

In all his songs, Barway Dorje appeals equally to our hearts and heads. He touches us—with his humility, his devotion, and his concern for others—while instructing and advising us with his wisdom and eloquence.

Yeshe Gyamtso

This translation is dedicated to
Tenpay Nyima, the Third Bardor Tulku Rinpoche

The Songs of Barway Dorje

A Collection of Instructions
Given to Fortunate Disciples
by Guru Vajradhara Barway Dorje

Namo guru vajradharaye!
The dharmakaya's sky is filled with the rupakayas' sunlight.
It dispels the darkness of beings' bewilderment.
To all the victors and their children embodied in one person,
To the feet of my peerless guru, I bow.

From the huge cloud of jewels that was his life
Fell a torrential rain of dharma deep and vast.
It soaked the dry soil of beings' hearts.
I will share this ambrosial garland of his secret vajra speech.

The great lord of siddhas, Jetsun Shepa Dorje, intentionally took rebirth as Karma Jikme Chökyi Senge Trinlay Kunkyap. He became the regent of Uddiyana, the second Buddha, and was called Pal Traktung Gaway Yeshe Dechen Barway Dorje Tobden Düdül Lingpa.[1] He sang innumerable deep and vast vajra songs to his many disciples from all places and traditions. Here are the songs that have survived in writing.

This detail from the thangka shown on the cover depicts the White Khechari. Painted by Terchen Barway Dorje, it is kept at Raktrul Monastery in East Tibet. Photograph by Bardor Tulku Rinpoche.

A Vajra Song of Awareness-Emptiness: A Prayer to the Great Revealer of Treasure, the Dharma King Urgyen Chokgyur Dechen Lingpa, Indivisible from the Trikaya Guru

E MA HO!
West of numberless worlds
Is pure Akanishtha, the Densely Arrayed.
In that realm endowed with five perfections
Is Samantabhadra, the protector Changeless Light.
He is none other than my guru's mind.
I pray to my guru, the dharmakaya.
Pacify my mind's thoughts of the five poisons.
Grant your blessing that my mind go to the dharma.

Far above us in this world,
In the renowned three lands of the gods,
Is the sambhogakaya teacher Vajrasattva.
He is none other than my guru's speech.
I pray to my guru, the sambhogakaya.
Purify the stains of my speech, channels, and winds.
Grant your blessing that I accomplish sound-emptiness speech.

In the south of India,
On the peak of Mount Malaya,
Is the nirmanakaya vidyadhara Vajradharma. Hear me!
You are none other than my guru's body.
I pray to my guru, the nirmanakaya.
Free me from my body's solid aggregates.
Grant your blessing that appearances arise as deities' bodies.

In various realms where beings are tamed
And in the cities of celestial realms
Are the five excellent vidyadharas.[2]
They are the treasury of all my guru's qualities.

I pray to my kind guru.
Purify my two veils and habits.
Grant your blessing that I realize luminous wisdom.

West of Jambudvipa,
In the glorious land of Chamaradvipa,
Is Padmakara, whose actions tame beings.
He is none other than my guru's actions.
I pray from my heart to the protector of beings.
Pacify the projections of our decadence.
Grant your blessing that the world be happy.

In the pure realm of the dharmadhatu,
In the palace of appearances' great array,
Is my guru of threefold kindness.
Tame my calloused heart.
Grant your blessing that my thoughts accord with dharma.

In the sky of the view beyond intellect
Dawn the sun and moon of luminous meditation.
The peerless garuda of conduct soars.
The knots of hope and fear about the fruition are untied.
For one's own good one is liberated as the jewel of dharmakaya.
From it come plentiful rupakayas for the good of others.
May I quickly accomplish this perfect fruition, the two bodies,
Glorious Samantabhadra.

This was the spontaneous prayer of the vidyadhara Dechen Barway Dorje, a disciple of the treasure-revealer Chokgyur Dechen Lingpa. May it bring virtue!

The Long Song of a Wanderer Describing Roads He's Never Seen[3]

Listen, children connected to me in the past:
Since you've persistently asked me to,
This wandering beggar will sing
Of the Buddha's teachings in the sutras and tantras,
Of the guru's guidance and the stream of instruction,
And of my bit of experience—
Just a seed, a reminder, a beginning—
Emulating the songs of our forefathers
And in examination of my being.

There are no words here meant to irritate anyone.
Turn your eyes toward this, forefathers!
This is the meaning of the tantras, commentaries, and the forefathers' teachings.
It might even help someone's practice!
Don't be competitive, my peers!
Understand my words.
You'll turn out more dharmic than me.
Don't fixate on my words, beginners;
Reflect on their meaning.
If you practice the essence of this,
It is certain that you will gradually discover the path of dharma.

From the beginning, rely on a guru who has good experience and realization
And whose being has blessing.
Through that, experience will arise in you.

The outer view and conduct of the shravakas and pratyekas, briefly put:
A timid cat roars a tiger's roar.
The cat wouldn't fool the great, fanged tiger,

But he's quick and agile; he eats meat and has claws.
He can overpower small animals.
He can at least find his own food.

The inner training of the mahayana:
When a dog barks trying to roar like a lion,
It doesn't sound too good to a lion,
But prudent people stay away.
The dog is able to guard the possessions of others.

The great, secret path of mantra and its result roughly put:
An eagle can fly to the peak of the wish-fulfilling tree.
Although it is certainly not as fast as a garuda,
The ocean of the two obscurations is dried to its bed.
The crown jewel of the naga king is gained.
Although the eagle is small, its wings are more powerful
than others'.

Everyone, listen to my song!
Its meaning bears the lineage's blessing.

The source of the pratimoksha is Rahula.
The sources of liberation through the bodhisattva methods are
Nagarjuna and Asanga.
The source of the river of the supreme vajrayana is Vajradhara.
From the blessing of father Naropa and Maitripa come
The dharma of the path of means and Mahamudra, the path
of liberation.
The family is unmistaken, the glorious Dakpo Kagyu.
These instructions come from that lineage.

Although the discerning don't need it,
Those like me should hear this.
The supremely learned who've achieved tolerance for
phenomena
And mere sophists—have a good laugh!

Children, make a song of it!
Youths, make a story of it!
Old men, make proverbs of it!
All men and women of this land, make an oral tradition of it!
All of you, make of it what you will!
If it displeases you, leave it alone!
All of the above is just rambling remarks.

E MA! The crown ornament of all existence and tranquility,
In this and all lives,
Father whose kindness could never be repaid—
I bow to the feet of the lord of all families.

You've seen what's wrong with samsara—suffering and affliction—
And have given rise to sadness.
Through the merit of pure virtue,
You've seen the benefit of blissful liberation.
The arising of renunciation is certainly the first blessing of the guru.
So that these bodies, hard to get, may be useful,
You have asked that I sing about the essential meaning
Of the heaps of dharma, rolled into one,
And the instructions left by past siddhas.

This humble, worthless beggar
Is as lazy as the village dog at home
But sought like gold elsewhere.
The three jewels led me out of the lower states.
My kind parents gave me this body, with leisure and resources.
The quintessence of the environment's four elements came together.
The motherlike lord guru
Lovingly nursed me with the inexhaustible treasury of instructions.
I drank the breast milk of the three vehicles.

I crawled at play in the fields of reading and the sciences.
I was put in the playpen of the outer shravaka and pratyeka yanas.
I heard the old men's tales of the inner mahayana.
I acquired the clever thinking which determined the truth.
I decided, for my own good, to conquer the single enemy.
Looking at the conditions, the appearance of external objects,
I sharpened the sharp weapon of knowledge.
I donned the armor of patience to prevent wounds.
I carried generosity as provisions to please others.
I wore saffron to fool everybody.
I summoned the desire for happiness as my companion.
I sent the fear of misery ahead as a spy.
I left the ruins of the eight consciousnesses behind.
I easily crossed the passes and valleys of dharma of the indicative meaning.
At the pass which separates superiors from the ordinary,
On the tower of the four noble truths, I hoisted the white silk flag of accomplishment
Through the power of past aspirations.
I found the testament of all the lord sugatas,
The final teaching of the supreme Shakyamuni,
The book of the factors of awakening
Written by the two noble chariots,
In which twofold selflessness was clearly taught.
I realized I had deceived myself.
I couldn't defeat the enemy externally,
But once this inner enemy, self-fixation, was killed,
The clouds of the eight consciousnesses vanished.
The afflicted mind's darkness was dispelled from its midst.
Externally, the moon of love and compassion shone.
Inwardly, the sunlight of bodhichitta spread.
Once ignorance, the hideout of the thief, was discovered,
Self-fixation, the thief, was caught.

All of his loot—the spoils of fixating on outer and inner
things as "mine"—
Was recovered.
The fortress of the eight dharmas was pulled down from its
foundation.
The root of all enemies was conquered then.

Then, I thought I should support my family, for the good
of others:
My father and uncles, the sources of inheritance;
My mother and aunts, who kindly cared for my body;
My spouse, to whom I was devoted;
My nephews and maternal uncles, my sources of counsel;
My paternal relatives and sisters, my supporters;
My brothers and friends, my companions in happiness
and misery;
And my neighbors, to whom I entrusted my concerns.
I supported them lovingly, fearing their misery.
I tried to please them, wanting their happiness. I tried and tried.
I gave them all the wealth they wanted and they still weren't
satisfied.
I spoke gently to them and wasted my breath.
I looked lovingly upon them and they never smiled.
I put food in their mouths but their bellies were never filled.
I caressed them with gentle hands and their expressions made
me shudder.
I loved them from my heart but their malevolence ran wild.
Forget about gratitude!
They became even harder of heart.
This is the complexion of our time; this is what's wrong with
samsara.
Our bosses are hard to please.
Our leaders exact a heavy tribute.
It is hard to take care of beggars and servants.
We are exhausted by the demands of our families.

We disappoint our mothers.
Our boon companions look askance at us.
All our neighbors bear us grudges.
If you have wealth, it trickles away; if you don't, you're poor.
If you have a retinue, they resent you; if you don't, you're stuck.
Those you help harm you in return.

So I threw off the enslavement of my family.
I came to view them as neither friends nor enemies.
I saw the pointlessness of all I had done.
I became certain that my enemies had been my parents in many lives.
I decided that my best friends were my enemies in this life.
Really, friends and enemies are no more than dreams born of habit.
When you awake, you laugh.
It's all an illusion that fools the eye.
The attachment and aversion of fixating on it all as what it seems to be
Is like a deer trying to drink the apparent water of a mirage; how could he?
You bewilder yourself through preference and prejudice.

This is what I have taken as the view, meditation, and conduct.
I barely make it into the ranks of mahayana practitioners of the paramitas.
However, my guru, Vajradhara, said, "You were definitely born into the ranks
Of practitioners of the profound and secret.
I empower you as a supreme vidyadhara."
He placed me on the three vehicles' throne of fourfold fearlessness,
And gradually bestowed the empowering anointments
From outer kriya all the way to the final secret.
He named me a king and crowned me.

He placed the emblems of means and knowledge in my hands.
He gave me the amrita of the secret empowerment to drink.
He bestowed the qualified consort for the path of the third empowerment as my queen.
He conferred the kingship of words beyond utterance.
He gave me the jewel, buddhahood in the palm of one's hand.
He appointed the paths of generation and completion as my ministers.
He gave me the protectors of samaya as my strong army.
Merit and wisdom became my elephant.
I ruled the kingdom of yogic discipline.
I established the land, the path of union and liberation, in bliss.
I collected the taxes of undefiled virtue.
With the example of past siddhas in mind,
And craving the lord victors' qualities,
I threw the golden wheel, the path of liberation, into the sky.
I rode the path of means as my steed.
I passed the royal lineage of blessings on to my children.
I placed the golden amulet of instructions at my throat.
I placed the many-colored robe of secret words on my shoulders.
I gazed upward with the eyes of faith and devotion.
I carried the sun and moon of unity in my hands.
Without falling into the abyss of samsaric bewilderment,
I turned the wheel of equal taste as means.
Not stuck in the narrow passage of the shravakas and pratyekabuddhas,
I soared like a garuda in the sky of dharmata.
I achieved the gods' victory of unbewildered buddhahood,
The ultimate state.
I simultaneously established all beings, my mothers,
Throughout billions of worlds, in bliss.
This is what I have understood and practiced
Through the kindness of the kind father guru.

I'm not proud.
This is what I've devoted myself to from the heart.
My words may seem boastful, but they convey the meaning
  of the texts.
This is unmistaken; it is the guru's instructions.
So, my children, please do this too.

Children I've nurtured with dharma for such a long time,
Because you've been blessed by many holy beings
Your veils are wearing thin.
You see a guru's qualities in this old man.
You've surrounded me with jewels and approached me
With flowers held between palms joined in devotion.
You've repeatedly prayed in request to me, saying,
"Oral instructions that will merge our beings with dharma,
And secret words of great import that come from your line,
  kind father —
You must sing a song that includes all of that."
You've offered me service of body and speech.
I must repay your kindness with dharma, by telling the truth.

This support of dharma, this precious body both free and
  endowed,
Is hard to get. Meditate on this through cause, image,
  and number.
Everything changes. Life is fragile.
Think how much like a candle in the wind is your life.
Pleasure and pain are caused by doing good and evil.
This is unfailing interdependence; believe it!
Competition with adversaries, favoring friends,
And the accumulation of wealth are a pit of unquenchable fire,
A prison, a nest of snakes, a razor's edge.
Consider that samsaric suffering never ends.

The rules of the outer pratimoksha

Are not merely a way to look good.
Don't let the major and minor rules taught in the books
Be lost in dichotomy between public and private.
They are the ground of a shravaka or pratyeka's path
  to freedom.
I pray from my heart that you keep them to the end.

Inner love, compassion, and bodhichitta
Are not merely a way to fool others.
Don't be fettered by selfishness.
Think of your mothers, all beings.
Help them with your three gates.
Resolve to place them all in perfect awakening.

The mahayana is the root of all paths.
Apply its profound mind training
To the taming of your own harshness.
We are enraged by the faults we see outside in others.
They are our own faults. Count them.
Clouds of the five poisons gather within our minds.
It is hard to see them without scrutiny.
Poisonous torrents and blizzards of agitation rage in our minds.
They kill the crops of our merit with their frost.
Please examine your being.

Faultless victors see all lower states
As realms of vaidurya
And all beings as sugatagarbha.
Tirthikas with impure minds saw
The Buddha as a mass of flaws.
All of you, exalted and common,
Consider your own faults and don't look at others'.

Our bewilderment in samsara's three realms
Is like the turning of a waterwheel.

There is unending change, birth, death, and migration.
The suffering of the six types of beings is unbearable.
Only the three jewels and the guru can protect us from it.
Take refuge in them with complete reliance.

Generate the two bodhichittas of the mahayana path.
They are commitment to the result and its cause,
And are like wanting to go and going.
Meditate on the four immeasurables until they mix with
  your mind.

With the four powers of a remorseful mind
Confess the three veils and all the karma
Accumulated throughout beginningless time.
Vow to stop it all.

Turn your body and all your possessions
Into a cloud of offerings like Samantabhadra's —
Both actual and imaginary—and offer them
In order to complete the accumulations.

There is far more profit to be made
In the industry of the seven branches
Than there is through selling bad food
Or making disastrous investments.

The truth is that all the splendid pleasure and goodness
Of samsara and nirvana are personified in the real buddha,
Your kind root guru and protector.
Always cultivate the devotion that brings down blessings.
Offer the pleasing service of accomplishment.
Venerate him by achieving his wisdom.
It is vital to see whatever he does as good
And hear whatever he says as dharma.

The common external preliminaries are the foundation of dharma.

Don't forget them or underestimate their importance.
The uncommon internal preliminaries are the life of dharma.
There can be no authentic dharma without this path.
Always and continuously implement them.

All points are included in devotion for your guru.
Don't let your mind get lost in scorn or fickleness.
If you see him as a buddha you've won.
If his blessings reach your heart you've both won.

The generation and completion stages of the actual path
Correspond to physical death, the interval, and rebirth.
To purify your ripened aggregates and elements
Cultivate the devakaya of the vase empowerment.
Get used to clear appearance that reverses solidity.

The channel-syllables, prana, elements,
Knots of impure karma, and winds of duality
Are tamed in the avadhuti's expanse
Through exercises and cultivation of the secret empowerment.

Everything is empty form like the eight illusions.
By integrating the illusory bodies of day and night
Tear fixation on appearances to shreds.
This is the monarch among ways to progress on the path.

The forward and backward flow of the drops bestow
Liberating means and great bliss—the upper and lower gates.
By perfecting the path of the four joys
Purify the ordinary pleasure of existence.
Reach supreme unity without transference.
Experience the third empowerment, the display of the connate.

Never moving from that ground, without mental engagement,
The lord of great bliss always resides in the bhaga of the lady,
Great emptiness with the best of all features.

This is the ultimate resultant clear light of great bliss.

From the very beginning they've never been separate.
Beyond permanence, termination, coming, going, decrease,
or increase,
All attributes of relinquishment, adoption, hope, and fear
are exhausted.
Gain full confidence beyond birth, death, or transference.
This method, chandali, is the pillar of the path.

Penetrate dreams in your throat.
Perfect the illusory body, emanation, and transformation.
Take this as the measure of the whole path.

Through eclipse and elimination at the heart
Develop the great clear light of the path.
When the clear lights of ground and path
Meet like a mother and child
All the paths and stages have been crossed
At once in the ultimate result.

Once you take birth, death, meditation, and dreams
On the path without bewilderment
You have arranged an escort for the interval.

The upper end of the avadhuti is the gate to liberation.
There are many techniques, such as trikaya ejection,
Transference, and sudden ejection. The most profound
Are reception through sambhogakaya ejection and
Diffusion in the dharmakaya through Mahamudra.
Learn how to apply them from your guru.

The point of all this is your mind.
Although it thinks lots of coarse and subtle thoughts,
Resolve that both thinker and thoughts have one ground:
Awareness alone.

Even when you look at your mind you can't see it.
It is inconceivable.
Don't tense up; it's clear when you relax.
That is its genuine nature.

The mere recollection of that is actual awareness.
There is nothing beyond that to see, even if you look.
There is nothing short of that to be found by searching.
The point is to simply rest in mere fresh awareness.

Even if your mind moves it is liberated in dharmata.
The ground of your mind is like a vast ocean.
Thoughts are like waves.
If they're not stirred by the wind of mental engagement
You never really stray from even placement.

Spy on good and bad thoughts while you're active—
Coarse and subtle thoughts of the six groups—
To ensure that you don't get lost in the ordinary.
Always cultivate gentle recollection.

The ground is the gentle current of even placement.
The path is the liberation of the streams of postmeditation
In that great river. When that occurs,
Even placement and postmeditation are indivisible.

Distraction to external objects is avidya.
Self-illuminating self-awareness is vidya.
This is the real difference between samsara and nirvana.

Don't wander in the valley of bewildered thought.
Please remain in the true fortress of self-awareness.

If you've not learnt much through the study of books
Try the method of bliss-emptiness, connate Mahamudra,
The wisdoms of the four empowerments, the path of devotion.

That is Mahamudra of mantra.

If you are learned in sutras and tantras,
Adorn your meditation with the Middle Way view.
Pursue the stages and paths of the paramitas.
That is Mahamudra for scholars.

These are the traditions of the peerless Daö Shönnu,
Called the Dictate-as-Instruction and Mahamudra
  Streams United.
This is the tradition of the father Kagyus.
There are many ways to enhance it through conduct,
But beware of the exhibition of signs of the path.
Don't crave samsara. Be in accord with dharma.
Accomplish the good of yourself and others.

Although my mouth spouts high and great dharma,
My mind is busier than anyone's
In its devotion to samsara.
Don't be a hypocrite like me.

Although my tranquil demeanor pleases everyone,
I conceal negativity within me.
My strategic exaggeration, denial, and ambiguity burn like fire.
Don't be ill-behaved like me.
Always be the same without and within.

We never reach the place we wish for.
We never get out of the pit we wish to flee.
When the bird is freed from the egg of ambition
Its wings of unity are fully grown.
It flies in the sky of nothing-to-gain.
No longer caught in the trap of hope and fear,
It does not search for the expanse of peace.
It does not land on the tree of bewilderment.
It gazes watchfully with eyes of compassion

On its mothers, the five kinds of baby birds.[4]
Spontaneously and effortlessly it raises them.
It owns the spectacle of samsara and nirvana.
What we call the result is no more than that.

If these rash utterances of this old man please you
Treasure them in your heart. As you asked,
I wrote as much as the paper would hold.
It is not meaningless talk.
Always read it and keep it in mind.
As requested by my son in dharma,
The devoted monk Drupwang,
This was written by Dechen Barway Dorje.
I pray that it be of use to all my disciples.
I dedicate this virtue to omniscience.
May the teachings of the father Kagyus flourish!

Until the End of Existence

NAMO GURU!
Until the end of existence I will bow from my heart
To the threefold vajravidyadhara
Whose kindness I could never repay:
My supreme guru.

You have good habits in your heart
And a connection through past aspirations.
You've said you need a song from me.
I'm busy but unable to refuse you.
I'll compose a song to help your mind.

When it comes to speech of experience I'm mute.
I'll make my point through images.
Amidst a gathering of Vedic singers
I'll sing a wandering tune.

Listen carefully, heartless people!
The essence of conversation is desire and hatred.
You've never faced up to death.
When you think of it you feel deeply depressed.

When young and old tough guys get together
They exchange tales of murder and theft.
They spend the day at play with dice.
They make a lot of pointless false promises.

We don't know where we'll go when we die.
Old people wasting their time in play is crazy.
Have you no hearts in your chests?

We don't know what good or bad karma we have.
When the old try to act young
They are tethering themselves to suffering.

A life spent at play ruins both the present and future.

It's disgraceful to ignore actions' results!
Think! Be sad in your hearts!

The young gather and sing with joy.
If they don't have cause for joy, however,
All their exclamations are in vain.

We accumulate a burden of gossip.
We fail to remember our suffering in this life.
We wait for opportunities to do wrong.
We are enticed by our lover—our kleshas—
And driven by maras—our bad karma.
Thinking of it, I feel sorry for you.

You are certainly worthy of better things.
Don't entrust your minds to such activities.
Engage yourselves in holy dharma.
Your father guru is certainly the scion of the victors.
Be the jewel of his heart.

If, following worldly custom,
You are enslaved by the eight dharmas,
You will become liars, scammers, and seducers,
More avid in the pursuit of profit, lawsuits, and investments
Than common people.
Spiritual friends of Mara are a bit disgusting.

It's said that the samaya of behavior
Corresponds to the three jewels.
However, merely clinging to the mark of the sangha,
Becoming like a river of apparently exemplary behavior
Spouting the foam and froth of jargon
Will not moisten the stone of your mind.
The driftwood of thoughts will pile up on the riverbanks.

The rapids of competitiveness will be turbulent.
The silt of kleshas will build up on the shore.
The view of mouth-only is a bit disgusting.

Since you don't know where you're headed
Your greatest resource, my disciples, is to view yourselves with honesty.
I pray to you all that you do.

Having rashly promised to be mantrins
You fail to apply generation and completion.
Your yidams are meat, liquor, and sex.
You let your kleshas run wild
And boast proudly of taking them on the path.
If anyone asks you about the generation stage
You reply, "The completion stage is the ultimate."
If anyone asks what dharma you've realized
You reply, "The point is benevolence."
Really, you're only fooling yourselves.
Your deceptive evasiveness is like the wind.
Mantrins like this are a bit disgusting.

The benefits and dangers of samaya are frightening.
Compassion for those like me wells up in me.
You say, "I am benefiting beings!"
You've never received the authentic four empowerments.
You don't even understand the meaning of the words.
You say, "I am bestowing the empowerment of secret mantra!"
Your buddies who've become your disciples
Receive the empowerments of ridicule and laughter.
They promise not to keep samaya.
You've made yourself and others samaya breakers.

Another activity in these dregs of time
Is the offering of shoddy tormas.

A master devoid of generation and completion
Is accompanied by a patron without samaya
In the performance of a ritual without beginning or end.
They bellow the forceful mantras of incorrect pronunciation
And attempt to "liberate" others without compassion.
They do more harm than good.

There are also those who say, "I'm a hermit who's renounced everything!"
Their addiction to the eight dharmas has steadily grown.
They meditate on the desire to be a lama and famous.
They abide in the state of relaxation and secret naps.

There are also those who say, "I'm a wandering renunciate!"
They lie to whomever they meet wherever they go.
They beat the dogs of every county with cudgels.
The knot of desire, hope, and fear burns like fire in them.

There are also those who've never scrutinized their mind's nature
Yet say, "I cultivate Severance!"
They fill the valleys with their bellow of PHAT!
Causing residents of the area to worry.

As I am sick of such views and conduct
I stay alone in the mountains.
In fear of losing my three gates to the ordinary
I've driven the stake of no-leisure into my heart.
Although I've not seen authentic dharmata
I've not lost the thread of recollection.
As I behave differently from everyone else
The seed of the habit of the three vows
Has not been cast into the abyss of carelessness.
I've retained the mark of our Teacher's followers.
The seedling of the training has grown within me.

I've investigated through a little hearing and thought
The path of causal characteristics, the pratimoksha and sutras,
The greater and lesser vehicles of the perfections.
Since I don't wear saffron or shave my head
I'm not an impressive hypocrite.
Nevertheless, I have carefully kept as best I could
The discipline of the mahayana pratimoksha.

My amount of precious altruistic bodhichitta,
Compassionate generosity, is not great.
It has proven difficult to be tranquil and subdued.
Nevertheless, I have never abused others in anger.
I have been as patient as I could.

Kinder than even the Lord Buddha himself
Was my father guru, my master.
I received the four seedlike empowerments of
The ultimate resultant vehicle, secret mantra.
I was never pretentiously submissive.
Although the subtlest rules are hard even to understand
I have protected like my own life, as best I could,
A simple sort of samaya.

As for the root, guidance through instruction,
I have not let it remain merely something I heard.
Although I've no signs of attainment to exhibit,
I've made a yidam out of the two stages' essence.

Although it's hard to achieve the full clear appearance of deities
I have through devotion gotten close.
Although I've not revealed the channels and winds
I've not been overpowered by my kleshas
And have been able to rely on the path of means' messengers.

Although I've not realized immaculate luminosity
I don't mistake the ground and path as separate.

I am comfortable with whatever arises naturally.

Whatever merit and virtues I have,
I've never desired fame or engaged in the dharma of vanity.
I've concealed my practice as much as I could.

Although I lack the realization needed to bless others
And the qualities needed to be taken as a guru,
I teach disciples devoted to me
Dharma that will help them according to their needs.
I've seen a few of them grasp the start of the path.
This is due to the kindness of the lineage of siddhas.

Without behaving like ordinary people,
I have worn white like the mahayana sangha of the past.
I have at least not wounded the doctrine
Of those who wear white and braid their hair.

Although I've been unable to undistractedly bring
The four states and four activities to the path,
I've not gotten lost in a chain of confusion.
I've achieved a little mindfulness through instruction.

I have nothing more than this about which to boast.
Nevertheless, I've never remained ordinary.
Even if I die soon, I'll be happy.
If I live for a long time I'll be even happier,
Because of my precious leisure and resources.

If you intend to emulate your father,
And want to be free of regrets at your death,
Recollect how hard it is to get precious leisure and resources.
Recollect death and impermanence.
Recollect cause and result, right and wrong.
Recollect samsara's suffering.

Take refuge in the three jewels.

Generate the intention to achieve supreme awakening.
Purify obscurations through the four powers.
Offer mandalas to complete the accumulations.
Your guru is a vast treasury of blessings.
Always cultivate the yoga of devotion for him.

Always apply with fortitude the path's
Two precious stages, generation and completion.

The Great Perfection is the ultimate path.
The spacious expanse of primordial purity is the limitless nature.
The ultimate resultant awareness appears as the vajra chains.
Through the interdependent means of the six lamps
And breakthrough into the expanse of the ground beyond intellect,
Cultivate from your heart this profound dharma.

Laziness is the greatest of maras.
Never forget to remind yourself to be vigorous.
Samsara is the procrastination of liberation.
Thinking about that, be disgusted.

Provide our kind parents throughout the three realms
With as much compassionate shade as you can.
Holy dharma is our only ambition.
Serve yourself in the way that will help you at death.
With benevolent aspirations and great courage serve others.

These instructions summarize the view and conduct
In a manner suitable for you.
Because of our past aspirations
We are bound together by a mutual affection
Greater even than that of father and son.
Although young, you have faith in dharma.
My karmic son, keep all this in mind.

This aimlessly wandering beggar
Wants to relinquish attachments.
Yet I miss disciples like you, my son,
With whom my connection is karmic.
I want to accompany you always, without parting.
However, this inactive beggar yogin
Returns at times to the place of his birth.
Then I wander off to other lands.
If I can, as I hope, stay alive,
I pray that, my son, we meet again.
Until then, my son in dharma,
May your precious illusory body be free from illness.
May your life force be as stable as a vajra.
I entrust your welfare to the gods.
May your wishes be fulfilled according to dharma.
These are the words left by a father to his son.
This is the holy dharma taught by my lord guru.
Make it an inseparable yidam in your heart.
These words composed as a song
Are the essence condensed for your use.
Son, don't forget this advice.
Through the connected aspirations of father and son
To virtuous, excellent, holy dharma,
May our wishes be auspiciously accomplished.

My disciple Padma Rinchen Dzegyen was born to a family of authentically divine origin. He has an excellent propensity toward dharma coming from previous training, and great faith in and affection for me. Presenting a fine gift of divine fabric and silver, he said he needed a song combining instruction and advice. Urged by him in that way, I, named Pal Traktung Gaway Yeshe Dechen Barway Dorje by deities and dakinis, wrote this. May it bring virtue!

Lord Guru Omniscient of the Three Times

Namo!
Lord guru omniscient of the three times,
I pray to you with fierce devotion.

I, an aimlessly wandering yogin,
Am sometimes a renunciate beggar.
I may not be a pretty sight on the outside
But I am ablaze on the inside
With the qualities of experience and realization.
This has not turned into vanity;
I cultivate devotion.
I've leveled fixation on pleasure and pain.
I'm utterly without hope and fear of high and low.
I've gained confidence in experience.
I'm happy to have few offerings to repay.
Really, I'm happy because my mind is at rest.

Sometimes I'm a noisy great lama.
I look affluent and smooth on the outside.
On the inside I am buffeted by the wind
Of craving for the eight dharmas.
I don't let it run wild; I bring it to the path.
I immediately cut through fixation on solidity
And craving fine things.
I've realized that apparent things are illusory.
I'm also without belief in nothingness.
When I get many offerings of faith I'm fine.
As I turn them into bases of merit I'm happy.

Sometimes I'm a fool acting crazy.
When people notice, there's a lot of gossip.
On the outside, I become a topic of conversation
For people both high and low.

On the inside my skill in bliss-emptiness
Expands in all directions.
As I can't force myself to pretend,
I've lost even the words "pretense of shame."
I have little hope for acquisition
And little desire for undeserved fame.

Sometimes I'm an eloquent teacher.
I please even the most argumentative people.
On the outside, they say of me,
"He has learnt how to lecture and write."
On the inside, I don't have much learning.
However, because I am not sectarian,
I can explain the view and meditation
In accordance with any tradition
And illustrate it through my own experience.

All my disciples who depend on me:
One: Don't call the three jewels to witness
Your rash declarations and schemes.
Two: Don't argue about tenets.
Three: Don't be obsessed with this life.
Four: Don't brag about anything you've done.
Five: Don't always talk about others' faults.
Six: Don't meditate on the difference between friends and enemies.
Seven: Don't be greatly attached to stuff.
Eight: Don't disregard causality.
Make these eight your constant yidams.

Other than this I have no advice.
If your devoted affection is not weak you are never
Separated for even an instant from your father guru.
We've met before; we'll meet again.
We'll keep on meeting as long as we live.

Gurus bestow the inheritance of samaya substances.
Disciples offer the service of devotion.
I offer my prayer that we meet repeatedly.
Since we are parting for a while,
I wish you every auspiciousness.

This was written by the wandering yogin Barway Dorje to his disciples.

Lord Vajradhara

NAMO GURU!
Lord Vajradhara, essence of the three bodies,
Father, root guru—I bow to you from my heart.

In this place with four changeless marks,
On the side of this mountain shaped like a horse's head,
On this ledge of rock, the Lion's Fortress,
Is someone whose behavior is that of a common, longhaired mantrin,
Who is, to call me by a nice name, a vidyadhara,
A yogin, if you look at my experiences,
A beggar who wanders aimlessly.
I will sing of external images
And of the inner nature.
I want, in my heart, to present offerings to the Kagyu fathers.

At first, I thought of the ocean of samsara.
Using the image of a boat to represent leisure and resources,
I dared to embark on a search for the jewels of meaning.

Second, I used the image of an illusory flower
To represent these changing aggregates.
I resolved that I was soon to die.

Third, I used the image of my hope for happiness and fear of suffering
To represent the causality of good and bad.
I chose what to relinquish and what to undertake.

Fourth, I used the image of work that will never end
To represent the subduing of enemies and the protection of friends.
I became utterly disgusted and nauseated.

I took the ground, dharmata, as the direct cause.
I took examining it as the indirect cause.
Because I've seen it directly, am I ever happy!

In its unlimited radiance, the appearances of samsara and nirvana,
I saw no three aspects—just appearance.
Is it ever luminous in the expanse of its nature!

Although this display of variety never stays put,
We stray into samsara by fixating on it as real.
But when I searched for what things arise from and dissolve into,
I ended up in the resolution of their emptiness.
The villainy of the thief—ignorance—was exposed.
The disastrous chain of mental formation broke by itself.
The rainbow of self-fixation vanished in the sky.

There was nothing in this ground that could be pointed out.
My path was to be free from the alteration,
Exaggeration, and denigration of whatever arises.
The sky beyond intellect was cloudless.
I basked in the sun, awareness beyond elaboration.
I took the moon, the experience of lucidity-emptiness, as a companion.
The planets of bliss-emptiness appeared in the background.
The stars of appearance-emptiness were innumerable.
Nonreferential compassion for beings, the unity of awareness-emptiness, was unceasing.
The forces of causality—adventitious, nonexistent appearances—
Were overwhelmed by the attack of beyond-the-limits-of-thought.
The royal palace of no-fixation was impressive,
But, as the person who gained it had no name,

Craving for its attainment was used up.
Because I saw that the attainment of the result is a mere
conventional isolate,
I was without any fear of falling back into samsara.
I saw the river of hope and fear dry up.

Now how happy is the meditating yogin!
This song of whatever experiences have arisen,
Sung in this place of blessing, this dwelling of practice,
Is offered to the holy tulku and his nephew,
To the faithful Anye Kuru and others,
To all who have provided resources,
To humans and nonhumans alike,
As an inexhaustible feast.
May you all play the music of delight.
This is unlikely to be an expression of realization,
But since the descent of blessings is uninterrupted,
I do carry the implementation of experience in my heart.
I dedicate meritorious virtue to beings.

While revealing the gate to the supreme place, Lion Sky Fortress, the vidyadhara Dechen Barway Dorje composed this spontaneously as it arose for him.

In Answer to Lama Jampal Gyaltsen

This was composed in answer to the questions of Lama Jampal Gyaltsen of Ga Nangtse while returning from a journey to Lhasa:

Courageous son of the siddhas
Bearing the flower of threefold faith in your heart,
With kind words of yearning
You've given this aimlessly wandering yogin
Who's returned from the central region
A feast of delights and stainless, fine scarves.
I'm pleased by this auspicious celebration.
You asked, "While wandering aimlessly from place to place,
What outer and inner wonders did you see?
Tell me of all in song!"
This old boy will answer your question.

From the original land of the ground, dharmata,
I saw the child of awareness set out,
Drawn by the illusion of appearances.
He entered the house of craving and conception.
He became exhausted climbing the stairs of formation.
Wrapped up in habits, he went to sleep.
When he awoke,
He became distracted by illusory appearances.
When his body, the form of bewilderment, had matured,
He played with the distractions of the six senses.

I was discouraged by the sight of birth
And came to despise the illusion of how we're born.
I put away the cause of birth
And sent forth the spy of no-birth.
I put him where he could spy unseen.
Now, I think I need not fear birth.

When the house of the composite is demolished,
And the rainbow of the body's four elements vanishes,
The dreams of pleasure and pain are experienced.
The old man who's traveled for so long is drunk.

I saw the difficulty of age and death.
Saddened by the sight of death,
I searched for supreme immortality.
The mist of this life and the next dissolved into the sky.
I entered the expanse, the impregnable fortress of immortality.
I saw that the designs of the composite were exhausted.
Even if I die right now, my mind is settled.

Those are the wonders I saw—birth and death.
These magical appearances are like a great optical illusion.
The bewilderment of the bardo is a clever deception.
These are all just like being fooled by a dream.

The spectacle of the six senses can include anything.
After the six senses and their objects have met,
The immediate mind takes over.
The great wind of the six consciousnesses blows.
The garbage of good and bad karma piles up,
Held by the net of the all-basis.
The result is the habit of samsara.
Temporary spectacles of all kinds can appear.
When the mind takes up pleasure and rejects pain,
The endless terror of samsara has begun.

But in the bardo between this life and the next,
The powerful hero, the clear light,
Rides swiftly on the steed of method, the illusory body.
He holds the sharp sword of equal taste
And the lance of yogic discipline.
He draws the bow and arrow of means and knowledge,
  bliss-emptiness.

He carries the provisions of samadhi.
He brings along emptiness and compassion as companions.
He is unafraid of temporary bewilderment.

This yogin, a warrior of awareness-display,
Went to central Tibet last year.
I was delighted by the sight of many supreme images.
I saw people from India, Nepal, and Kashmir.
I met supreme incarnate lamas, masters,
And the great sanghas of dharma foundations.
In Kyishö a female spirit created illusions.
In Tsethang I met terrestrial dakinis,
And at Gampo, Gampopa himself.
I saw a mandala in the sky of Tsaritra,
And, in a town there, a ganachakra of place-born dakinis.
I met the celestial dakinis all at once.
I taught causality to maras and barbarians.
In Zangri, I saw the dakini Machik Lapdrön
Dancing in sambhogakaya form.
In a dream in Flower Field
I heard predictions in the sound of a stream.
In the Spirit Lake of the Empress of the Desire Realm
I saw her wondrous palace and park,
The wild swirling of a black wind,
And her mule trotting to and fro.
At the gate to Tsangrong, I saw Thangtong Gyalpo,
White like a conch, the size of a mountain.
In sacred places, at passes, in valleys, on mountains, and by lakes,
I saw innumerable yidams, dharmapalas, male and female protectors,
And more—in meditation, in dreams, in pure perception, and in my mind.
I received countless predictions.
In Yömo I saw a feast of heroes

And received predictions from place-born dakinis.
That is a summary of the wonders I saw.
But I also saw assemblies of faithful disciples,
The directionless conduct of yogins, and more—
All the wonders of the whole land.

I like singing songs of equal taste.
It is amazing that the deer of our bewildered minds are drawn to
The mirage of the appearances of this life.

I have seen still other wonders:
The charnel grounds of the sacred places in external appearance
And the cities of dakinis within the internal channels and winds!
I have tasted the ganachakra of the protector dakinis.
I've seen, I've seen, I've seen and not seen.
Really, I've seen there is nothing to see.
I've seen the nature of the buddha of ground.
I've seen the appearance of bodies and wisdom.
I've seen wonders beyond exaggeration and denial.

Really, while this yogin wandered through the land,
While I went to all those places,
Only boundless purity appeared to my mind.
I never experienced anything impure.
Beyond that, the visions, pure appearances, and clear
  appearances
I experienced in those places are too many to recount.

In this context of human birth,
These are the appearances to my undistracted six senses.
These are the outer and inner wonders I've seen.
Your question was sincere, so I've answered it honestly.
I have sung this for everyone,
Although the suspicious may call me a charlatan.

That is this yogin's spontaneous song,

An offering of talk about the nature of things.
Please take it as enjoyable music.
Through the virtue of this, may all beings of the three times
Acquire the seed of awakening.

In answer to the questions of the supreme siddha, Lama Jampal Gyaltsen (the heart-son of the holy guru, the Lord of Siddhas of Nangtse) this was dictated by the one given the names Pal Traktung Gaway Yeshe Dechen Barway Dorje and Tobden Traktung Nakpo Düdül Lingpa Tsal by deities and dakinis to the scribe and monk Losal Prajna. MANGALAM BHAVANTU!

This Beggar, This Yogin

A HO! This beggar, this yogin—I, Barway Dorje—
Went to see the sacred places in the middle of the land.
When I was at the seat of the glorious Lord Tsalpa,
At the end of the night, in the last of my sleep,
While my mind was a mix of sleep and clear light,
I saw a beautiful realm in the west,
In it a mountain and on its peak
A three-storied palace of jewels
In a tent of rainbows.
In the center of this transparent palace,
On a lovely and precious throne, lotus, sun, and moon,
I saw seated the glorious Avalokita.
This was mixed with the sight of central Lhasa itself,
Which spontaneously appeared as a pure realm.
I gained conviction that the Lord Dalai Lama, Vajradhara,
Is Avalokita himself.
The victors, our refuge, emanate through compassionate skill.
They manifest inconceivable variety for the taming of beings.
This is hard for the foolish and infantile to fathom.
So don't make partisan distinctions;
Let your devotion be impartial and all-inclusive.
May all keep this in mind.

This is our ensuing conversation written down as a song. At the repeated request of Ringul Lama Jampal Gyaltsen, this was composed by Barway Dorje. Virtue!

Lord Guru and Deities

According to the wishes of the lord of siddhas, Yudrak Tulku, father and mother, an amrita accomplishment of the *Guru and the Eight Dispensations* was convened at the supreme place, Yudrak. During it, the following was composed in answer to the questions of the mother Sukhadhari:

Lord gurus and deities, omniscient of the three times—
I pray to you with devotion's yearning.

The various evils of these dregs of time sadden me.
Yet through the compassion of my kind gurus, my refuge,
And through the blessing of the Lord Padmakara,
We have assembled here in order to gather the accumulations
and purify obscurations.

This is one of Tibet's twenty-five sacred places.
At the foot of Yudrak, the sacred site of Kyura,
This temple contains the three jewels.
The tulku vajra-holder is the leader of the yogins.
His consort is Sukha, so generous with all she has.
These two brought together the food, funds, and place.
Last year, that of the ox, I and seven tulkus and lamas,
With more than a hundred and fifty male and female monastics
and laypersons,
Performed a *Vajrakila* great accomplishment,
And this year the amrita accomplishment of the *Guru and the Eight Dispensations.*

During these, in visions combining meditation and dream,
I have been accepted by Shriheruka.
The glory of summer has flourished here.
The matrikas and dakinis have gathered like clouds.

Flowers signifying excellence have fallen like rain.
All the dakinis, those with bodies and those without,
Have joined the birds in the sky above.
I have heard the mantras sung by the dakinis of space.
I have heard the secret language of the heroes of the five families
Buzzing like bees,
And have seen their playful dance of spontaneous appearances.

What we have done here has meaning.
We have accomplished the happiness of beings in this place.
We have served the secret mantra teachings.
This old man goes from place to place;
Here I have done something genuinely great.

In answer to the request of the consort, Sukhadhari,
I, Dechen Barway Dorje, offer this.
May all of you—father, mother, and children—
Live long and benefit beings.

External Appearances

The following was offered as a small flower of words in answer to another request by Ringul Jampal Gyaltsen:

External appearances arise as my yidam.
The internal mind-itself is realized as my guru.
On top of Nangtse, the second Potala,
I offer this flower of euphony
To the supremely diligent Lama Manjushri.

A HO! Without thinking anything, everything is mind.
If you think of everything, there isn't anything.
If your mind is not isolated from elaboration,
Isolation of body and speech are merely temporary.
Isolation of mind is the child of the childless,
Merely a name, without essence.
All elaborations are pacified in the expanse of no-elaboration.
From the state of no-elaboration anything can arise.
Mind and appearances are not two.
Without meditation there isn't an instant's distraction.
Bliss-emptiness indivisible is Mahamudra.
If you don't fixate on the elaborate,
How can you fixate on the unelaborate mind?
The unelaborate is an all-pervasive spinning wheel.
The bonds of elaborated characteristics
Are cut by the sword of wisdom beyond elaboration.
Once the net of samsara, nirvana, and the path has been torn apart,
The great hidden flaw of cause/result and good/bad is exposed.
Natural, spontaneously present—A LA LA!

This was offered by that common mantrin from Tashi Surmang Lhundrup Ling.

To Your Lotus Feet

To your lotus feet I bow, wish-fulfilling jewel.
Dharmakaya Yogini, bless me!

You bring joy to all who live.
You have understood all outer and inner things.
With homage of the three gates, I respectfully address
The lotus feet of the guru with eightfold mastery.[5]

As medicine for eyes afflicted by this fivefold degeneration,[6]
You have appeared, according to your wishes, Yishin,
In a supreme form like a sky-jewel, Norbu,[7]
The full mandala of marks and signs.
I am greatly inspired by your rescue of disciples.

I am well but use up the result of past virtue
By chasing after poisonous offerings and wandering through villages.
I tell myself this is altruistic, but it is really just selfishness.
I feel sorry for myself, but there is nothing to be done.

Nevertheless, at all times in this bardo of birth and death,
Having cut through the complexities of the three times, I remain at ease.
I rest easily in the unaltered nature. The dream of thoughts,
Like the child of a childless woman calling to the east and west
From the top of a mountain, is over.

I sit slumped, having resolved that all these appearances are illusions.
Things have no nature. I drink the saliva of elephants
From a begging bowl made of rabbit-horn.

In a single meditation session, this yogin of simplicity
Ended all the complexities of this life.

With not a speck of anything to do, I put on a saffron blanket
Woven from tortoise-hair.

If you have no hope or fear, you have no need for fruition.
That which is attained and the attainment of it are purified,
Like the ornamental kamala flowers of the sky.

I have written this as a design in a dream,
Employing the four impossibilities as images.[8]
May it be a pleasing offering-cloud. PUJAH HO!
With the prayer that we meet again soon, with divine fabric,
And with the two precious things, this was sent from the monastery and offered
By the one with threefold perception called Raktrul.

Composed in a Crowd of Playful Youths While Wandering Through the Town of Kundröl in Upper Ga

The sky-jewel of the guru's blessing
Has appeared in the lotus garden of disciples.
As I have followers it's time to sing tunes.
I do have some fine honey of instruction.

I've heard the good news of a perfect spring.
Beings of the six types are like a herd of beasts.
Spiritual friends are like herders protecting them.
Kleshas are like a mountain blizzard.
The three bad migrations are like talk of wolves.

Herders, cast aside sleep and distraction!
Bring your herds to the pasture of worthy virtue.
There, they can graze on rich grass and flowers.
They will bleat the MANI's six syllables.
They will lie down in the pasture of well-used leisure
  and resources.
Shout the KI and SO of holy dharma.

The unfortunate, like pigs, will flee from you, herders.
They will eat filth, trash, and mud.
They will disturb others with their grunting.
They'll wander off a precipice in search of wealth.
Stop them with stones of compassion.

They'll run as a group from the horns of impartiality.
When the sun of dharma rises they'll run into the rocks.
When the rain of dharma falls they'll hide in caves.

Their tongues crave the salt of kleshas.
They are filled with restlessness.

Hit them with a stone from the sling of means and knowledge.

When they see the herder they play with him.
They lie and say they've seen what they've not.
Like infants they don't understand what they see.
They are in conflict with goodness; such is behavior in
  bad times.

They lie and say they've heard what they've not.
The vulgar don't understand what they hear.
Benevolent talk is impossible anywhere.
It would be better to recite MANI.

This unaltered child, Barway Dorje,
Lacks the glamour to please everyone.
I've made a few benevolent aspirations.
Whether connected to me by good or bad,
Those with faith, pray to me.
Those without faith, denigrate me.
My bodhichitta makes no distinction between these.
I don't discriminate between good and bad among my parents.
I generated bodhichitta in front of my guru.

Young men and women, sing this song.
It bears the interdependence of liberating this whole land.

I composed this in the midst of a group of young people who were singing in the town of Kundröl in Upper Ga. Virtue!

From East of Jambudvipa

I sang this spontaneously through great sadness when I saw monastics and laity gathered in Tridu overpowered by their obsession with this life and chasing the mirage of bewildered thoughts:

From east of Jambudvipa
Has come the golden sun.
It has warmed the elements
And illuminated the four continents' darkness.

It's not that dark now.
Even if they're in a dark hole,
The fortunate are reached by this light.
Yet the blind are isolated in darkness
That is hard for anyone to dispel.

The great wind of Vishnu's locks
Has come from the land of devas.
Like the rishi's daughter
It has moistened the three worlds.

Hard iron and jewels
Are melted by red fire,
But base grim stones are not liquified
Even when immersed in water.
How could they melt in fire?

Unrolled peas are rounder
Than a hundred rolled pellets.
Unsharpened thorns are sharper
Than a thousand sharpened weapons.

Daytime's bad habits
Become bewilderment in dreams.

Dreams' good habits
Bring happy days.

The advice of an old man of divine lineage
Is even better than dharma.
Youths of evil lineage
Are born but never grow up.

The slowly flowing Tsangpo River
Is the source of precious gold
From which are made the three supports.
The wake of a golden fish
Is a right-spinning joy-swirl.

The king of mountains Mapang
And lordly Sepongnam
Are chief among all devas in this land.
They bestow good fortune and siddhi.
I step on my enemies' necks.
My activity spreads in all directions.

This child of the Mukpo Dong
Is a Fearless Lion of Dharma[9]
On the snow mountain of the siddhas.
I'm proud of the turquoise mane of tradition and realization.
The brains of the little clawed animals of incorrect thinking
Are crushed by the iron claws of reason.

This call of melodious song
Is medicine for youthful sadness.
This yogin who wanders the land
Is a friend who cheers you up.

From within a colorful great monastery
Comes the resounding call of the horns.
On the pale path of circumambulation
Maidens dance playfully.

Will the monks be lost or not?
It depends on their individual minds.

This yogin has no boss and no lackeys.
I'm only concerned with the future,
So I will bow and circumambulate.
I care nothing for present appearances,
So I'll visit the local tavern.

In a little cave among the rocks
The hermit seals his door with mud.
In isolation, without noisy distractions,
Dharma can really begin.
By raising the banner of accomplishment
He serves as a good example.

The beggar who practices Severance,
Bellowing HUM and PHAT
And biting his lip at spirits,
Has not subdued the demon of his own mind.
He's become just like someone
Who goes around beating up dogs.

Fine silks and brocades
And pretty things of gold and silver
Are okay if they're placed on your head
During an empowerment.
Nowadays the best we can do to help beings
Is assemblies with "great blessing."

Beating great drums
And filling their bellies with meat and liquor,
They shout, "Kill, kill, strike, strike!"
They toss magical weapons of fire and water.
They are not aimed at a target.
Who knows whom they hit?
Who knows whether all this helps or hurts?

This seems to be the fashion in ritual.

Meanwhile, homeless men and women
Without even food or clothing
Recite the good names of buddhas
And quietly murmur their MANI.
Few give them anything to eat.

Learned bodhisattvas
Wise in deep dharma
Give little sermons
To which few lend their ears.

Most people are drawn to charlatans
Who shout in spirit tongues
And beguile their listeners.

What a wondrous spectacle
Is the savage custom of our time!
The yogin Barway Dorje
Is going to wander aimlessly.
If you bump into me once,
Don't hope to see me again!

Think about yourselves.
That should end in tears.
Once you lose your independence of thought to others,
You no longer own your own mind.
Who would dare brag about that?

Root guru, know!

The rest of you, without faith in your hearts,
Have a nice dance!

I composed this in the midst of a lot of people who were in denial of death and impermanence.

In This Northern Land of Snows

This was composed at a feast of playful maidens from Dzongpo and Mering:

NAMO GURU!
In this northern land of snows,
A place tamed by Great Compassion,
An unending series of victors have come as protectors.
We all sing the six-syllable MANI.
Our minds burn with devotion for our gurus.
We are blessed and uphold dharma.

I offer this feast of a six-legged warrior[10]
To the smiling lotuses of your minds' threefold faith,
Playful maidens of this place.

Wearing delightful ornaments worthy of the gods
You surround the swanlike vidyadhara.
Blessings appear like the six-legged ones' dew.
I sing the sound of deep dharma.

This king of swans named Barwa
Prays that the playful maidens of this place
Are compassionately blessed.

From the Expanse of Great Bliss

Composed as oral instruction for women of Palkhyim Yedrong gathered in play:

From the expanse of great bliss atop your heads
Your kind root guru sings to you of dharma.
Smiling with pleasure he plants the seed
Of freedom in the fortunate with faith.
Pray with yearning and no doubt.

I am deeply saddened
By our endless bewildered planning
In this inescapable ocean of samsara.
Give up worldly actions.
Emulate the lives of siddhas of the past.
I offer the benevolent aspiration
That I lead all connected to me to freedom.

Composed by Barway Dorje for some women of Yelpa.

The Ground is Empty Mind-Itself

Instruction given to the woman of family from Tridu named Ayu, who has affectionate faith beyond separation:

The ground is empty mind-itself.
The path is unaltered nowness.
The fruition is unchanging unity.
The view is samsara and nirvana without good and bad.
The meditation is clear light beyond the intellect.
The conduct is immaculate, without relinquishment
and adoption.
The fruition is the exhaustion within the expanse
Of thoughts of the three aspects,
Something to get, and someone who gets it.
Through thoughtless aspirations the two wisdom bodies
Blaze like wish-fulfilling jewels
With the splendor of existence and tranquility.

That is the root verse. The difficulty of acquisition of leisure and resources; death and impermanence; the results of actions; and the defects of samsara are the roots of achievement of the path's qualities. Meditate on them earnestly. The essence of the path is ceaseless devotion for and prayer to your guru, who is kinder to you than all buddhas of the three times. The pillar of the path is diligence. With diligent freedom from distraction, repeatedly renew recollection in all situations. The impediments on the path are doubt, cynicism, excessive physical activity, endless conversation, speculation and thought about the three times, and too many concerns. Relinquish these as much as you can by relying on their remedy, contentment.

All our samsaric strategies surrounding food, wealth, clothing, jewelry, houses, land, protecting our families, and suing our enemies; our desire for greatness, fame, and nobility; and our concern with the eight dharmas ruin our virtuous intentions. Do not harbor the demon of selfishness. Cultivate disgust—feeling deeply tired of samsaric endeavors—as a branch of the path. As it is the means of liberation from this samsara, which is like a prison or a filthy swamp, think within the depths of your heart, "I must definitely accomplish holy dharma!" You must in any case establish fierce renunciation—accompanied by thoughtful reflection upon the danger of bad migrations—as a basis.

To progress on the path, generate vast compassion and precious bodhichitta for those who have not realized that all things are like dreams or magical illusions. Be never without the benevolent intention to bring vast benefit, both temporary and ultimate, to all who have been your mothers. If your mind turns purely to dharma, even if you suffer during your brief human life in these bad times it will not matter because you will be concerned only with benefit in future lives. This attitude is excellent under any circumstances. Keep this in mind, all of you! Why would this old man, whose intentions are wholly benevolent, not rejoice in this? I pray that no matter what happens you all prevent your human bodies from going to waste and accomplish your own benefit.

In response to the request of Tseyang, a devoted woman with affection for me beyond separation, this was written spontaneously by Barway Dorje. Virtue!

Unfailing Refuge

Instructions given to a dakini of family, descended from Urgyen Chokgyur Dechen Lingpa:

NAMO GURU!
To the unfailing refuge, the three jewels;
And my kind protector, my root guru:
To you who are all-sufficient
I bow from my heart.
Grant your blessing that I remember impermanence and death,
And that I apply dharma to my being.

Hard-hearted people who take their lives to be permanent
Never notice the destruction of composite things.
May they perceive impermanence and be freed from the bonds
Of fixation on the permanence of substantial entities.

The environment and its contents are formed and destroyed.
The four seasons also pass.
Years, months, days, hours, minutes,
Daytime, and night pass moment by moment.
Given that, how could these flesh-and-blood
Aggregates and elements last?

The vajra body of the lord Samyaksambuddha
Has gone with the wind.
I've never seen a siddha who didn't change bodies.
How could these piles of vomit,
Our bodies, be permanent?

This illusory body is borrowed from the elements.
It quickly wilts like a flower.
We are adrift in the waves of birth, aging, sickness, and death.
Since we could sink at any moment,

What good is it to pretend that life is permanent?

In any person's life there is much pleasure and pain.
In one life span there are many ups and downs.
Where has the time from the day of your birth until
  today gone?
You don't know; it's been consumed in distraction.
If you think of it now, you wonder.

Few die in old age.
Many die young.
Life is breathing.
Will your last breath be in or out?
How could you live after that?
Once the force of good karma's used up,
Even if your body were made of iron it wouldn't help.
To speak of a long life is self-deception.

All composites are like waves on water.
They are never still; one follows another.
Death is like drawing straws;
You never know who will get the short one.

Our families are like fellow shoppers at a market.
We are soon parted.
With different karma, we go different places.

If you have dharma, death is just a dream.
If you've done great wrongs, there is great regret at death.
If you're always benevolent toward others,
Gently spoken and harmonious,
You will die at peace and happy.

If you have generation, completion, and virtue,
In one instant you will achieve perfect buddhahood.
How could such a death be anything but a delight?

Your mind is emptiness, without any birth or death.
If you just rest in it without distraction,
You will accomplish at once great good for yourself and others.

Friendship, however intimate, does not endure.
Constant company leads to great quarrels.
We see our friends' virtues as flaws.
We despise both the best and the lowly.
We are arrogant about helping others.
Even if others behave well we see them as wrong.
We denigrate everyone without distinction.
Watch out for these behaviors.

Give rise to faith in the three jewels.
Bear your guru, your refuge, on your head.
Cast meaningless conversation behind you.
Cultivate present self-awareness, liberation through recollection.
Recite the six-syllable MANI, liberation through hearing.
Rely upon samaya amrita, liberation through taste.

Give up thoughts and actions harmful to others.
Do as much for others as you can in thought and deed.
Give up resentment and jealousy in your heart.
Be benevolent; spread goodwill.
In all you do be in accord with dharma.
This will help now, later, and always.
Never forget this; practice it.

In your mind, emptiness, there is never birth or death.
Even if the external world is destroyed, your mind is unharmed.
Even if your internal illusory body is lost, your mind has
  nothing to fear.
Your mind resides in the fortress of immortality.

These words have meaning.
Their meaning is the intention of all victors.

They are jewels for faithful hearts.

This little song about meditation on impermanence
Is this old father's word of the heart
For a woman of divine family.
I dedicate it to the realization of the unborn essence.

In response to the encouragement of the woman Paldzin Lhamo, this was hurriedly dictated by Barway Dorje at the foot of the supreme place, Jewel Crystal Rock, to the scribe Karma Lodrö Rapten. May it bring good in all ways!

Beyond Repayment

When my disciple, the monk Karma Dulwa, was living in solitude I wrote this to remind and encourage him:

NAMO GURU!
Beyond repayment is your kindness in all my lives.
I pray to you, my root gurus.
You've given up your own good in undertaking others' good.
I bow from my heart to you, victors and your children.

Listen to this brief explanation of the three wheels
Of view, meditation, and conduct
For a humble yogin who has generated
The benevolent intention to practice dharma.

Whatever happens from now on in this life,
Samsaric endeavors will never come to an end.
We are blind, stunned, out of ideas.
Don't you regret the mistake we made in the beginning?

Although you now think in your heart,
"I must definitely accomplish dharma that will help later,"
You are uncertain how long you have left to live.
Oh, oh, this precious leisure and resources!
Although we know better, we are mindlessly distracted.
Don't you regret having wasted your life?

If you want the permanent happiness of yourself and others,
It is time to give up all this negative thinking.
It is time to stop all these samsaric endeavors.
It is time to start thinking for yourself.
It is time to focus on the essence, holy dharma.

Isolation will not hide you from death.

It will, however, enable you to give up negative distraction.
Our forebears have taught us to accomplish dharma in retreat.
It is time for you to live in mountain caves.

Subduing enemies and favoring friends are the tethers
That pull us down into bad migrations.
It would be better for you now to subdue your five poisons.
Gaining fame through ill deeds is a never-ending occupation.
If you subdue ignorant self-fixation, you're truly tough.
If you've no craving for these appearances, you're truly smart.
If you accomplish the ground of others' benefit, you're truly classy.
If you give up malevolence, you're truly learned.
If you want unmistaken success, cultivate holy dharma.

First, know the rarity of leisure and resources.
Second, remember impermanence and death.
Third, don't mistake the results of actions.
Fourth, give up distractions if you want freedom
From samsara, this pit of fire and nest of snakes.

Your guru embodies all buddhas of the three times.
Take refuge in him and purify obscurations
Through the power of his compassion.
To gather great accumulations unreservedly offer
The mentally adopted, the imaginary, your three gates, and all you possess.

All victors treat all beings as their only child.
Gather great accumulations by meditating
On the giving of your happiness
And the taking of beings' suffering.

If you really believe that he embodies all buddhas,
With devotion for your root guru as their embodiment
And unbearable yearning, totally mix your mind and his.

Whether you're happy or miserable, regard it as your
guru's compassion.
Whether things are good or bad, regard them as your
guru's qualities.
Carefully make all your behavior accord with dharma.

There is no enemy other than ignorance.
There is no help other than unaltered awareness.
There is nothing to do other than remaining undistracted.
There is no obstruction or samsara other than distraction.
There is no tranquil buddhahood other than no-distraction.

Methodically abandon your faults.
Energetically accomplish all good thoughts and deeds.
Always be very kind to yourself.
Take care of your loved ones nobly with dharma.
Meditate on compassion for enemies as for your mother.
Stop denigrating the praiseworthy, praising the unworthy,
And harming anyone, good or bad.
If you can, help even your enemies.
Never do anything to harm anyone.
Always call your mind to witness.
Change your deeds of body and speech
By changing how you think.

In your external conduct, accord with the nirmanakaya's
commands.
The precious pratimoksha is the ground of all qualities.
In your internal cultivation, accord with the samboghakaya's
teaching.
With inviolate samaya know your aggregates and elements as
deities.
Secretly, never be without bodhichitta.
Very secretly, accord with the dharmakaya's teaching, the
Great Perfection.

With external, internal, alternate, expanse, and awareness all indivisible,
Cultivate without error the profound instructions of your guru.

Don't desire rank; it's empty space.
Don't desire fame; it's a vanishing echo.
Don't desire comfort; it's like drinking salt water.
Don't harbor great desire in your mind;
It's like the invisible wind moving the grass.
Decide to accomplish holy dharma now.

Give up mundane companions; rely on wisdom self-appearance.
Mundane food never satisfies, no matter how much we stuff our cheeks;
Enjoy the food of samadhi in even placement.
Mundane clothing will not warm us in the cold hells;
Warm yourself with the supreme heat of chandali.
Tie up the ends of mundane appearances.
Wish for rest in the ultimate bliss of peace
As the thirsty wish for water.
If you always keep this in mind, you will accomplish much.
No matter how long your cultivation of holy dharma goes on,
Don't give up. These are words from my heart; keep them carefully.
Always keep the inexpressible in mind.

For the retreat of Karma Vinaya,
My longtime dharma son,
These instructions were composed as they occurred to me
By the old father Barway Dorje
At the Lion Fortress Hermitage blessed by Guru Rinpoche.
I pray that this may reach the minds of yogins on the path,
And that it may be properly cultivated.

SARVADAKALYANAM BHAVANTU

Instructions on Purification for My Disciple Targyay Gyamtso

NAMO GURU!
I bow to the supreme guru Vajrasattva.
I will provide here a little instruction for disciples
On the purification of karma.

Imagine your guru, Vajrasattva, above your head
In the form of the second Buddha, Padmakara.
In nature he is Padmakara indivisible from your root guru.
He is white and red with one smiling face.
His two hands hold a vajra and a kapala of amrita.
In sambhogakaya attire, he is embraced by white Tsogyal.
Seated in vajra and lotus posture, they blaze with light rays.
They are sitting on a lion throne, lotus, sun, and moon.
They clearly embody all buddhas of the three times.
Offer a billion mandalas, your body, and your possessions.
Confess all wrongdoing of body, speech, and mind of the
three times.
In their heart on a moon is HUM surrounded by the hundred
syllables.
Streaming amrita purifies wrongs and obscurations.

Recite the six syllables, the hundred syllables,
And the all-sufficient VAJRA GURU.[11]
Pray to Guru Rinpoche and the three roots.

Your mind, awareness of this moment,
Is beyond characterization as this or that.
Without being distracted from the continuity
Of mere presence, cultivate it without fixation.
Whatever happens—birth, death, joy, or misery—
Remain undistracted yet relaxed.

Always entrust your heart to your root guru through devotion.
Turn your mind to holy dharma.
Give up as many mundane actions as you can.
If you do all this, you will accomplish much.

It would be excellent for you now to engage in purification and accumulation according to tradition, with inviolate samaya toward both your guru and your monastery, entrusting your whole life to the cultivation of virtue in a good retreat in isolation or in a hermitage. Please keep the tradition of doing so in mind. Written by Barway Dorje. May it bring virtue!

Instructions for Palkhyim Arme Urgyen

These are instructions to aid the recollection
Of my faithful disciple who wants liberation.

Now, later, in between, and in all situations;
While walking, standing, lying, and sitting—in all activities—
Imagine above your head whomever you want to,
Such as your root guru, the protector Amitabha,
Avalokita, or Guru Padma.

Pray with devotion and yearning without a moment's lapse.
Offer without reservation your body, possessions, wealth,
Retinue, spouse, children, and the four continents.
Repeatedly gather the accumulations.

Amrita streams from your guru's body,
Purifying wrongs and veils.
Light rays from his five places dissolve into you.
Think that this purifies the veils of the three gates and their unity.

Your guru melts into light and dissolves into you.
In the indivisibility of your mind and your guru
Rest without a care but with self-recognition.
Don't adopt stillness and reject movement,
Seeing one as good and the other as bad.
Apply yourself repeatedly to mere self-recognition.
Such meditation is the ultimate practice. Keep it in mind!

As requested by Arme Urgyen,
This was quickly written by Barway Dorje.

From This Time On

In the supreme place of accomplishment, Khyijam Lion Fortress, I restored through pure appearances the succession of ripening and liberation through the Golden Dharmas of Dharma Lord Barompa's Oral Lineage. At that time I composed this vajra song as a declaration of realization:

NAMO GURU VAJRADHARAYE!
From this time on until supreme awakening,
Infallible refuges, three jewels,
Present in one, omniscient Vajradhara,
Glorious, mighty Padma—I bow to your feet.

The kind ones who are not other than him,
Lords known as the sun and moon,
The holy father Kagyus, accepted me.
This is not mere worldly convention.
They introduced me to Mahamudra.
They did this repeatedly, not just once.
They gave me direct instruction like a pointing finger,
Revealing it suddenly, so that I saw whatever arose in its nakedness.

They are the protector Tilopa, a human buddha,
Who united the rivers of the four dispensations;
The glorious, blessed Naropa and Maitripa;
The supreme Hevajra, the translator heruka;
Lord Mila, the source of the lineage of accomplishment;
The protector, the single ornament of Jambudvipa, called
 "physician,"
The origin of liberation, who united the Middle Way and
 Mahamudra;
His disciple and heart-son, the peerless, glorious Barompa—
Is he not Lord Tarma Wangchuk?—

The lineage holders and dharma sons of that supreme one,
The Lords Tishri and Sangwa Rekar;
The holder of the ultimate lineage, Lume Dorje;
And all those in the beautiful, golden garland
That holds the essence of amrita, the river of the profound, secret dispensation.

In the sky of glorious Kirtidhvaja
Shine the sun and moon, the protectors Mati and Punya.[12]
Their disciples and disciples' disciples are shining planets and stars.
The brilliant light of the sun never sets.
It warms the lotus of previous karma.
Bees are nourished by its nectar.
The moon, dispelling darkness, circles the four continents.

Now is the time when interdependence's design
And the changeless imprint of this line shall appear.
The supreme Vajra Queen appeared as a human woman in this world
As Namkhai Naljorma, the dakini of the expanse.
In the monastery of terrestrial Akanishtha
She appeared in the attire of a samaya dakini
In order to accept me.
She bestowed, complete in one, the instructions of the oral lineage,
The profound import of the tantras, and symbolic empowerment.
I wondered if I wasn't following the tracks of the father Kagyus.
I gained immeasurable faith and joy.

In this supreme realm, present from the beginning,
The glorious Heruka and hosts of dakinis have gathered like clouds.
The herds of siddhas and vidyadharas have blessed us.
Those with and without form have gathered here.

It is like the rock from which a great lion leaps into space.
He surpasses all mundane predators.
The siddha abiding here is victorious.
He has tamed the haughty with his fangs and claws of a lion.
His power of a lion has grown from within.
He displays his turquoise mane and white coat to the ten directions.
There will be powerful lion cubs.

The blessing of the father Kagyus is great.
The river of supreme instruction continues to flow.
I sit at the end of the lineage ranks.
Although the power of my knowledge is not great,
I have not fallen from the sky with an extreme view of the ground.
Although my diligence in the means of meditation is slight,
I have unified the sun and moon in the path of luminosity.
Although my courage in yogic discipline is not great,
I have engaged in the conduct that is the means of unification.
Although I lack qualities pleasing to others,
I have found the result, buddhahood, within myself.
Although it's hard to tame a mind like mine,
The fever of desire has vanished with age.
My weakened mind has lost the teeth of anger.
I surrender victory to the competitive.
I avoid confrontation with the jealous.
I don't much crave wealth.
I may not behave well, but I try to avoid inappropriateness.
That's my true story.
Because I know myself I can say
There is nothing hidden that could be exposed.
Why should I exaggerate my qualities?

All my disciples from now on:

Know that the line of instructions from glorious Naropa
and Maitripa
Is superior to others in its profundity.
This profound path, prophesied by the dakinis,
Comes through a short lineage.
At this time, the end of the third five-hundred-years,
The environment is changing as fast as a field in spring.[13]
The kleshas of its inhabitants are like dust in a tornado.
Their behavior in this decadent age moves like the wind.
Thinking of this, I cry.

Remember the lives of the father Kagyus.
It's time to relinquish the ambitions of this life.
Meditate according to the instructions of the oral lineage.
Hurry up and practice supreme Mahamudra.
All disciples who depend on me,
Don't waste your lives through capriciousness.
Apply your minds to practice.
Don't procrastinate; hurry!
I wish for the interdependence to meet repeatedly.

That's my answer to my sons' request.
In the pleasant valley of Kyijam, on the bank of the Drichu,
In a place like a great lion leaping into space,
In a spacious cave like the lion's mouth,
I, the last son of the father Kagyus,
Pal Jikme Chökyi Senge,
Have spoken from my heart for the benefit of you disciples.
May the teachings of the ultimate essence spread!

Yudra Nyingpo, Karma Kagyu Tashi, the young woman Kachö Drönma, Jomo Khyi, and others were the first worthy, fortunate disciples to receive this dharma. In response to their common request, this was spontaneously composed by Dechen Barway Dorje, Karma Jikme Chökyi Senge, at the supreme place, Lion Fortress.

Glorious Heart-Sons of the Three Times' Victors

In repayment of the kindness of my disciples, such as the holy supreme emanation Karma Gyamtso and the yogin Karma Döndam, I composed this song about the attainment of certainty regarding the view and meditation of Mahamudra:

GURU NAMAYE!

Glorious heart-sons of the three times' victors
From that uncomposed expanse beyond elaboration
That pervades all like space—
That self-illuminating expanse radiating compassion—
You are the shining suns that dispel ignorance's gloom.
Your compassionate light rays extend in all directions.
I bow to my root gurus.

All you worthy disciples gathered here!
This old man was resting at ease when you said,
"Sing us a little song of advice
That will be good for us now, later, and always!"

I'm just a foolish and humble old man.
As I'm not learned in worldly deeds,
I never made it into the ranks of clever men.
I gave up on competition and nepotism.
I've spent half my life as a beggar.
As my brain's not bursting with machismo,
I've been relegated to the end of the line of the lowly.

The lord victors' compassion, however, is impartial.
Their eighty-four thousand dharmas are resourceful.
My father gurus' compassion is not weak.
My spiritual friends have been very kind.

Although I fell into a field of dharmic instructions,
I'm still just a weak and timid old man.
My understanding through study's not great.
I've no qualities from training.

Since I can't compete even with those who appear well-behaved,
Forget about scholars and siddhas!
It would be hard to place me among monastics.
I stuff myself with the burning coals of undeserved offerings
And waste every day of my life in idleness.
I'm devoted to stupid sleep all night.

For an old man whose whole life has been like that
To advise others while lacking experience
And to speak of divine dharma while lacking training
Is like talk of a raven's teeth.
It will make a great story later on.

However, as I am so old,
I do possess experience both good and bad.
I do know, I think, the meaning of joy and misery.
Solely so that I not refuse your request,
I will pull a meaningful song out of my crazy words,
And present it to you brothers and sisters gathered here.

Within any mundane activity
It is far better to behave nobly.
As taught by the protector Nagarjuna,
There are sixteen pure human dharmas.[14]
If properly cultivated with benevolence
They become the ground of all virtues,
Since human dharma and divine dharma are one.
These are the seeds of all virtue.

If you can give up the ten wrongs,
The external dharma of shravakas is there.
If you can cultivate the six causal perfections,

The root of the bodhisattva vow is complete.
Based on the ground of the four immeasurables,
If you apply the means of generation and completion,
You possess the samaya of supreme secret mantra.

Clever disciples, old and young,
If you've brains in your heads you're the best.
Please remember the rarity of leisure and resources.
If you remember this in your heart, you've a useful body.
Urge yourselves with impermanence and death.

Actions' results mainly come from good or bad intentions.
From great Vajradhara all the way down
To a bug on a blade of grass,
No being is beyond karma.

All causality is included in good and bad intentions.
You know yourself best.
Please give up, like poison, ill intentions.

Although we can't judge others' minds,
Fulfill others' wishes. Be benevolent.
Do whatever helps others.
Please think and act with your heart.

Whoever cherishes others more than themselves is the victors' child.
There is nothing better than that.

Although the great secret vehicle's ocean's depths
Are beyond fathoming in their profundity,
The point is that cultivation and samaya are the same.

The refuges—the three jewels and three roots—
Are the play and dance of a single mind.
All samaya is included in the root guru.

The ground of benevolence is spacious.
In it grow the crops of the six perfections.
The samaya tree's rooted in that ground.
The fruits, the trikaya, ripen there.
The point—the root—is bodhichitta.

This stainless ground of sugatagarbha
Is said to pervade everyone,
From buddhas and bodhisattvas all the way
Down to beings in bad migrations.

This mind, this tathagatagarbha, fills outward appearances,
Our bodies, and our hearts.
We can't say "It extends just this far" or "Here it is,"
Just as we can't find the ends of space.

It never comes or goes. It never stops.
It is beyond the elaborations of the three times,
Even placement, and postmeditation.
It is the middle beyond the four ends.
It is the Mahamudra that fills all experience.
It is the Great Perfection, the ground complete within us.
It is not composed and therefore not composite.
It is an expanse without essential existence, the dharmadhatu.

This is the real view, self-illuminating self-awareness.
If the expanse of this unchanging ground does not fluctuate,
This is meditation.
If there is no adoption and rejection, this is instruction.
If the sun of unfluctuating brilliance shines
In experience but without fixation,
This is the result beyond hope and fear.
Attainment and attaining have been cast into the expanse.
Really, the view and meditation are just this.
The conduct of samsara and nirvana is spontaneous.
It is drinking the honey of existence and peace.

Disciples, it is without adoption and rejection.

Accumulate as much virtue as you can.
This will accomplish the seed of the path of accumulation.

Search for your mind outside and within.
No matter where you look—throughout existence, peace,
All parts of this world, its inhabitants, and your body
From the top of your head down to the soles of your feet—
Your flesh, bones, veins, the pores on your skin,
Your innards, lungs, heart, its blood,
Your senses, and their objects—
You will never find anything about which you can say,
"This is my mind-itself!"
That is original emptiness.

Understanding this, experiencing it, and realizing it
Are called lesser, intermediate, and greater one-pointedness of mind.
By continuously cultivating familiarity with this,
Means—self-arisen devotion—will burn like fire.
You will see your protector, your guru, as an actual buddha.
Unbearable compassion for beings will arise.

Through blessings entering your heart,
The fog of experience will vanish like a rainbow.
You will shed, like a snake, the old skin of subject and object.
The ruins of hope and fear will be demolished.
The thief of self-fixation will be caught and killed.
The lie of samsara and nirvana will be exposed.
Elaborations will be severed without.
The sun of no-elaboration will dawn within.
The mist of hope and fear will vanish in the sky.
Although your mind does not elaborate on doing so,
It has landed on top of no-elaboration.

The stages and means of the path are complete.

Like the first sight of the waxing moon,
Your mind, the only buddha, is first encountered then.
This is said to be experienced in an instant.
This is said to be the path of seeing, the first level.
The perfection of this realization and its qualities
Is called lesser, intermediate, and greater no-elaboration.

Your mind's wisdom is displayed like a magical illusion,
Without clinging or fixation,
As the spectacle of all the external world's appearances.
You see them without craving them.
Their variety is all contained within the expanse of one taste,
Like an illusionist regarding his various illusions.
Although they have no nature, they seem to exist.
Although they appear, fixation has broken down.
Although they appear, seer and seen are broken.

Like a dancer looking at herself in a mirror,
Like writing words without language,
Like following a bird's tracks in the sky,
The first seven levels of the path of meditation are completed.
This is what is renowned as the path of training.

Through the yoga of the path of the four mudras,
You reach the final level. However,
Like describing a road one's never traveled,
Anything I say about it will be both vague and disconnected.

Although it's unfitting to speak overconfidently,
Really, samsara and nirvana are complete in one.
In the state of mind where the three times are equal,
There is no difference between buddhas and beings.
How could we ever appraise

The qualities of the kayas and wisdoms?
Effortless awareness is unceasing.
The aspects of union are naturally complete.
Self-awareness and great bliss are inseparable.
The path beyond training and the three pure levels
Are said to be quickly completed.

That's enough of this old man's rambling.
None of this was book-learnt or thought up;
I've said whatever occurred to me.

Now, you said you needed instructions for death.
Your body has four states.
Don't try to patch them with thought.
Your mind is tathagatagarbha.
It is without the elaboration of three times.
Therefore death does not really exist.
Our illusory bodies are just like old clothes.
We put them on; we take them off.
Like the clothes you wore in a dream last night,
How could you take them to be lasting?

Birth is like the child of the childless.
Can you speak of that child's growth or education?
It is always like the eight images for illusion.
Everything merely seems, to your bewildered mind, to exist.
Nevertheless, relative causality is unfailing.
That is the dharma of the nirmanakaya sugata.

Your channels, winds, and drops are a victor's body.
Wherever you are is a palace and pure realm.
It has always been innately thus.
Since it is, recollect it as it is with clarity.

All the men and women in the world
Are embodiments of sugatagarbha.

They are all yidam gods and goddesses.
Since they are, experience them in their actual purity.

With an undistracted mind, let your hair turn white.
Toothless, recite dharma.
Aged, still dance youthfully.
Accomplish your own good in this life.

Now, very old men like me talk wildly.
You youngsters have up to now in your lives
Succeeded in every dharmic and mundane endeavor.
Still, look up to this decrepit old man.

Apply yourselves in changing bad mental habits
And especially in self-cognizant awareness.
You will be like my children in this old man's mind.
Those who know how to think, keep this in mind.
Those who don't understand it, don't ridicule it.

This little song in answer to your request
Was composed by the old man Chökyi Senge.
My clever son Karma Gyamtso wrote it down
With fingers that move like lightning,
Smiling to himself the whole time.

May you disciples and all beings attain omniscience
Together with this old man.
May the Victor's teachings spread and flourish.
May the greatest dual benefit be quickly accomplished.

The Rarity of Leisure and Resources

While traveling along the Dri River I presented these instructions to my disciple Sönam Tobgyal:

KYE! If you know the rarity of leisure and resources, you are clever.
If you meditate on death and impermanence, you are wise.
If you choose actions through knowing their results, you are learned.
If you meditate on the defects of samsara, you are erudite.
If you tame thoughts and kleshas, you are tough.
If you accomplish altruistic wishes, you are noble.
If you can accumulate and purify, you are wealthy.
If you can be independent in dharma, you are exalted.
If you recognize your own mind's face, you are mighty.
If you've no regrets at death, you're a warrior.

KYE! Even if the foolish are praised by their enemies, they are nothing special.
Even if the dharmic are reviled by their friends, they have no regrets.
There is no greater profit than the accomplishment of small virtues.
There is nothing easier than the giving up of small wrongs.
There is no refuge for now and later like your guru.
There is no samsaric tether like your home.
There is no way of life like holy dharma.
Therefore, think about yourself.

KYE! When away from our guru we forget the dharma we've heard.
When amidst many people we forget our own mortality.
When distracted by amusements we forget the need for virtue.

Through laziness we forget the need for accomplishment
in retreat.
Through apathy we forget the passing of our lives.
Through sleepiness we forget to pray to our gurus.
Through meaningless conversation we forget to recite the MANI.
Through desire we forget the samaya of secret mantra.
Through anger we forget to cultivate patience.
These dangers exist; be diligent!
Don't forget your guru now; pray like this:

NAMO GURU!
Single father, holy guru,
Emanated dancer, tamer of beings,
Great treasure-revealer, king of dharma,
Urgyen Chokgyur Dechen Lingpa,
Father, mother, and your children—hear me!
Better than the buddhas,
Peerless in your kindness,
Traktung Gaway Yeshe
Dechen Barway Dorje—
Take hold of this devoted child!
In these dregs of time, this age of dispute,
Your lineage has passed to such as me.
Father, look upon me with compassion!
In this red-faced crowd devoid of dharma
I've luckily found a dharmic body.
I have no other parents.
Your single child is crying.
Lead this lucky child to the path.
I am begging you in desperation!
I am praying to you with longing!
Look, look upon me!
Quickly grant your blessing!
I've no other hope than you!
Be of genuine help to me!

Free me, I beg you,
From inescapable samsara.
When I am menaced by kleshas,
May the militia of wisdom be alert.
Transform into pure deities
This illusory body's degraded aggregates and elements.
Release into emptiness's expanse
The knots of klesha channels.
Release into the pure avadhuti
The karmic winds of subject and object.
Through the blissful wisdom of melting white and red,
May I complete the levels and paths of the four joys.
May I master the ultimate chandali of great bliss:
The karma, jnana, and supreme mudras.
Through the application of wisdom
May I presently refine the clear light,
Overcome the habitual delusion of dreams,
And master emanation and transformation.
May the six illusory intervals
Be transformed into pure deities.
In the trikaya's expanse of great bliss
May the ejected, ejection, and target
Be brought to their original purity.
In all my lives, care for me without separation.
Show me the way to liberation.
Unmistaken holy guru,
This child takes you as a father.
See me as your child.
On the samsaric paths of the six causes,
We wander in the darkness of bewilderment.
Bring me—your child—and all beings
To the land of omniscient freedom.
We are a flock of the blind.
Guide us on our way.
From now until awakening,

We have no hope other than you.
Guide us to the end.

Recite that prayer repeatedly with longing.
Think of me continually, day and night.
For the whole of our lives
We remain uncertain where we're going at death.
Who has ever been misled by holy dharma?
Therefore, thoughtful people, think about this.
I may be a heap of exaggeration and denigration,
But I've the aspiration to free all connected to me,
Whether that connection is good or bad.
I vow to you that I do not divide
My children into good and bad.
If we fail to help ourselves,
Only our gurus will help us.
But if we fail to cultivate devotion,
We turn from samaya to denigration.
I've seen a lot of this.
Therefore, please, no matter what, help yourself!

In response to the exhortation of my disciple Sönam Tobgyal, I began this by writing down whatever occurred to me. After writing the first four lines of the prayer I heard what I believe to be the voices of my glorious guru, the victors, and their children saying, "We will bless your children who pray in this way." Feeling confident, I, Traktung Gaway Yeshe Dechen Barway Dorje, completed the prayer with references to the profound six dharmas.

The Essence of All Instruction

The essence of all instruction is diligence.
Keep the holy dharma taught by your guru in your mind.
Now, while you can think and understand,
Count your actions, right and wrong.
Choose now either perennial happiness or suffering.
Contemplate the rarity of leisure and resources, death and impermanence,
Adoption and rejection based on cause and result, and disgust for samsara.

The main thing is: Where did your mind first come from?
Where is it now? Where will it go in the end?
The environment, its inhabitants, outside and inside your body—
Where does it go? Where is it now? What are its shape and color?
Searching, you don't find anything. Rest in that emptiness.
If intellectual fixation arises, rest evenly on top of it
Without artifice or alteration.
A variety of experiences—elation, depression, clarity, obscurity, and such—
Will occur. Don't hope for or fear them. Cultivate what is there.
Having gradually achieved the experiences of bliss, clarity, and nonconceptuality,
You will quickly attain the wisdom of the path of seeing.
Cultivate devotion—completely entrusting yourself to your all-sufficient guru—
And unbearable compassion for all beings who've not realized this.
Cultivate diligence—ensuring that your three gates never stray into the ordinary—
And disgust for samsara as for a prison.
Through such meditation, experience and realization will gradually arise.

As requested by Arme Sönam and Kunga Gyaltsen, this was written by Pal Traktung Gaway Yeshe Dechen Barway Dorje. Virtue!

Primordially Pure Nature

Om ah hum!
Primordially pure nature, the protector All-Seeing;
Spontaneously present character, Outshines All Seals;
Compassion at play, Barway Dorje—
I pray to you. Ripen my being. Liberate my three gates.
May dual benefit be spontaneously accomplished.
May I quickly achieve the state of the Stable Wheel.[15]

My mind has never, from the beginning, been born.
It is emptiness, does not abide, and will never stop.
Appearance-emptiness, awareness-emptiness, and
clarity-emptiness united,
Its nature is fresh awareness of the moment.
Unaltered, unsullied, it is beyond removal, addition, rejection,
and adoption.
If it remains natural, beyond concepts and the intellect,
One is never without the cultivation of no-distraction
In even placement and in bringing postmeditation to the path.
This is the instruction through which a son emulates his father.

This was written for the devoted disciple Atra
By his old father Barway Dorje.
I dedicate its virtue to all beings' realization of unity.
May this bring virtue! Sarva sujaya![16]

I Salute the Root and Lineage Gurus

I salute the root and lineage gurus!

If, my child, you want to practice Mahamudra,
Cultivate its preliminary, devotion Mahamudra,
And the undistracted Mahamudra of this present awareness:
The first moment's unaltered freshness.

Don't settle, patch, alter, or speculate, "Is it or isn't it?"
Don't split hairs in doubt.
Relax within whatever arises, merely remaining present.
Do no more than that. Don't fix or alter anything.

This was quickly written by Barway Dorje
For the disciple Tashi Döndrup.
May self-arisen Mahamudra be quickly realized!

Unfailing Three Jewels

Unfailing three jewels, refuges;
And my kind root guru—
Thinking of you, I cry constantly.

If you want to accomplish the greatest good for yourself
and others,
Meditate with unbearable devotion for your guru.
Knowing these beings to be your parents,
Cultivate as much benevolent compassion as you can.

When your mind recognizes itself,
Don't choose between stillness and movement.
Don't hope for clarity and fear obscurity.
Don't hope too much to see.

"Unbound, ordinary cognition" means
Unaltered, natural cognition.
It is unbound, left to itself, through mere presence.
Cultivate this through constant diligence.

Know that we never complete
Our inexhaustible samsaric schemes.
It's best to let go of craving.
If you want dharma, have fortitude.
Fear wrongdoing. Give it up as much as you can.

This was written by old Barway Dorje
For the disciples Lekden and Tamdrin,
To encourage diligent accomplishment.
I offer my aspiration that your thoughts accord with dharma
And that you be without obstacles.

Lord, Buddhas of the Three Times in Human Form

Lord, buddhas of the three times in human form—
I bow from the heart to my protector, my root guru.
Grant your blessing that having acquired a body
With leisure and resources and having met dharma,
I apply dharma to my being.

Since it is impermanent and destructible,
What use is it to hold life to be permanent?
May I give rise to unremitting diligence
And the devotion of complete trust
In my holy guru, the unfailing refuge.
My mind that thinks this and that
Is misled by ignorance.
May I cultivate like a river's current
This fresh self-aware cognition.

Lord, protector, kind root guru,
Glorious Dechen Barway Dorje—
I pray to you from the depths of my heart.
Father, hold me in your compassion.
Mix your mind with mine.
Now, later, and in between,
Embodiment of all refuges,
Noble lord, hear me!

This was written by Barway Dorje for Könchok Shakya, Gema Tsulzang, and other disciples. May it bring virtue!

Looking at Your Mind

"Looking at your mind" means this:
When you become aware of various thoughts, good and bad,
Use that very awareness to look suddenly at your mind.
That awareness is unaltered and fresh. Cultivate it.

Afterward, whether your mind is still or moving,
Don't pick and choose. Give up your desire for stillness
And your dislike of movement.
Cultivate mere presence of mind.

Don't desire something better or higher than that.
Refrain from intellectualization.
As soon as awareness is present,
Other than cultivating its mere presence
There is not a speck of anything to be done. Have no doubt!

In the same way, whenever you are distracted,
As soon as that sudden awareness is present,
Just cultivate it without alteration.
It is what's called "fresh awareness."

The essence of all instructions is to cultivate it
While walking, while sitting, and in all activities.
Always cultivate as much devotion for your guru as you can.

This was written by Barway Dorje in response to the repeated request of Gönpel and Tsering. May the unmistaken ultimate nature be seen!

I Bow to Those Lords, My Root Gurus

I bow to those lords, my root gurus.

If you want to cleanse the wish-fulfilling jewel of your mind
With recollection and awareness;
If you wish to receive from that jewel the siddhi of all you need,
Pray with unbearable devotion to your guru,
All of the three jewels personified.

As it is the root of all dharma,
Cultivate with unaltered awareness
The fresh mind of the moment.

Give up the desire to see something and the hope of clarity.
Have little fear of obscurity and unknowing.
Cast aside thoughts of doubt and passivity.
Don't cling to experiences of bliss and clarity. Destroy them!
Give up boredom with the taste of no thoughts.

Within whatever thought arises,
Cultivate your mind as it is without removal and addition.
Doing good and abstaining from wrongdoing is the best conduct.
You will accomplish the result through freedom from hope and fear.

This was written for Karma Nyendrak
In a cabin at Lion Fortress
By Pal Traktung Barway Dorje.
May ultimate Mahamudra be accomplished!

Empty and Clear, Its Nature Awareness

Empty and clear, its nature awareness—
Just cultivate that. Give up intellectualization.
Don't desire insight or clarity. Cultivate what's natural.
Devotion and disgust are always friends of the path.
Apply this and you'll accomplish something great.
Urgyen Gyamtso, keep this in your mind!
Barway Dorje wrote this in Yudrak.

My Guru, All Buddhas of the Three Times

My guru, all buddhas of the three times,
I pray to you with fierce devotion.

Cultivating, without hope, fear, or alteration;
And without choosing between stillness and movement,
This mere recognition by your mind of itself
Amidst whatever arises is the essence of cultivation.

Always pray to your guru
And have compassionate benevolence for beings.
Dedicate all virtues to beings' benefit.

This was written for the faithful Tsega
By Barway Dorje. Virtue!

All of You, Cultivate Your Minds' Freshness

All of you, cultivate your minds' freshness without distraction.
Always pray to your lord guru.
Recite the king of secret mantras, the VAJRA GURU.
Don't mix up right and wrong.
You'll definitely accomplish buddhahood.

Written by Barway Dorje.

When Your Mind's Careless and Distracted

When your mind's careless and distracted
Apply awareness to your mind-itself.
Cultivate awareness through mere alertness.
This fresh awareness recognizes itself.
Don't get lost in conceptual appraisal.
Letting go, whether there is stillness or movement,
Cultivate mere recognition, mere presence.
Don't appraise or force anything.
Meditate on devotion for your guru,
And on death and impermanence.
This was written for the disciple Dargyay Gyamtso
By Barway Dorje. May there be virtue!

All the Three Jewels Embodied

OM AH HUM!
All the three jewels embodied, dharmakaya, the victors' mind;
The eighty-four thousandfold speech of all the three roots;
And the mind of a hundred samadhis and a million wisdoms:
I pray to my guru of immeasurable qualities.
Grant your blessing so that my mind may see its own face.
Single refuge amidst degeneracy, emanated from
  Guru Rinpoche's mind—
I pray to Dechen Barway Dorje.
May I be held by your blessings.

May my mind—unborn, momentary awareness—
Know itself in unaltered freshness.
Cultivating that without alteration, contrivance, or appraisal,
May I be free from choosing between stillness and movement,
And from hope for the good and fear of the bad.
May I not be polluted by the intellect.
Resting freely in whatever arises,
May the blessing of knowing how to cultivate this enter
  my heart.
Grant the blessings of devotion for my guru, compassion for
  beings,
Disgust for samsara, recollection of impermanence and death,
Knowledge that good or bad intentions
Are the principal determinants of actions' results,
Caring more about others than about myself,
The taming of my negative being,
And the accomplishment of benevolent thoughts and deeds.

Always undistracted, may I never forget mere presence.
May I ceaselessly recite prayers, the VAJRA GURU, and the MANI.
May I always make good aspirations of dedication.
May my mothers, all beings, attain buddhahood.

May I have a long life without illness and accomplish virtuous
dharma.
May I finally become indivisible from that buddha, my guru.

In response to the wishes of Arme Sönam Wangyal and the young woman Kalzang Lhamo, this aspiration was made by Dechen Barway Dorje. May it bring virtue!

You, My Disciple

You, my disciple with genuine good intentions,
Don't crave the busy distractions of this life.
Continuously recollect impermanence and death.
Spur yourself, from your heart, on the authentic path.

If your guru's blessing doesn't enter your heart,
It is hard for dharmic qualities to arise in your being.
Pray, therefore, to your root guru.

Rest freely in the freshness of your mind recognizing itself
Without the ignorant alterations of the intellect.
Whether there is stillness or movement,
Just cultivate mere no-distraction.

Never pollute it with "I'm doing this," "I will do that,"
Desire for clarity, hope for the good,
Dislike of obscurity and movement, and other fears.
By cultivating this you will accomplish your great goal of
liberation.

This was written in a moment by Barway Dorje
For the disciple Tenpa Dargyay
At the request of Dechen Gyalpo.

Personification of Blessings and Wisdom

Personification of the blessings and wisdom
Of the three jewels, three roots, and all victors;
Dharma Lord Traktung Dechen Barway Dorje:
I pray to you. Bestow the supreme and common siddhis.

All gurus are embodied in Guru Padmakara.
All yidams are embodied in Arya Avalokita.
All dharmapalas are embodied in Vajrakila.
If you always keep them as yidams there will be virtue now
and later.

Based on always acting for others' good,
Be diligently undistracted from the gleam of awareness:
Fresh, unaltered mindfulness.
Guard your samaya and vows like your eyes.
Always behave harmoniously toward all, high and low.
Make benevolent aspirations and dedications for all.

At the request of the women Manibhadra and Könchok Chözang,
This was written by Barway Dorje on a virtuous day
For all women of accomplishment.

Glorious Embodiment of All Buddhas

Root guru; glorious embodiment of all buddhas;
Heart son of Padmakara, the buddha of the three times;
Dechen Barway Dorje; Düdül Lingpa:
I pray to you. Bestow the supreme and common siddhis.

In this freshness the guru and self-awareness are indivisible.
Knowing how to see the face of Mahavajradhara
Through unaltered, self-arisen devotion,
May I accomplish the fruition of buddhahood in one life.
This was written in a moment by Barway Dorje
For the woman Devadaki.

First Tame Your Continuum

First, tame your continuum with the four common dharmas.
Second, take refuge, purify, and accumulate.
Third, meditate on guruyoga in four sessions.
When devotion becomes authentic, blessings will enter you.
Effortless realization will appear automatically.

NAMO! Kind and compassionate, you ripen and free my continuum
Through transmission, empowerment, and instruction.
You embody all root and lineage gurus.
Beings' protector, Mipam Trinlay Kunkyap,
Jikme Chökyi Senge: I pray to you.[17]

Grant your blessing so that renunciation may arise in my depths.
Prophesied by the *great splendor blood-drinking* deities,
Celestial lord, *joyous wisdom*,
Your body is the union of *great bliss* and the best aspect.
With a *blazing vajra* you crush the head of ignorant thought.
I pray to the *powerful*, *mara-taming revealer of treasure*.[18]
Bless me so that my continuum accords with dharma.

Bless me so that kleshas and bewildered thoughts
Are purified in dharmata's expanse; pleasures, not abandoned,
Are brought to the path; and the supreme fruition
Of the five wisdoms and bodies is accomplished in this life.

Without alteration or fabrication, gently rest your mind-itself
In fresh awareness of whatever arises,
Without craving, fixation, or activity.
Relinquish doubt, the thought "Is this it or not?"
Don't desire knowledge or insight.
Without thought give up whatever happens.

These are the instructions of Traktung Dechen Barway Dorje
For Lama Karma Gönpo.
I pray for your spontaneous accomplishment of dual benefit.

To Cultivate Your Mind's Nature

Tutor, to cultivate your mind's nature,
Do not be content with your understanding of emptiness.
Diligently cultivate, as much as you can,
Unaltered even rest in the fresh nature of whatever arises.
I have no instructions beyond that to give.
Written by Barway Dorje at the wish of Tragyal.

When Mind-Itself is Caught by Awareness

When mind-itself is caught by awareness,
Don't introduce the speculation "Is this it or not?"
Don't wonder. Don't think. Rest freely.
In postmeditation cultivate naked awareness,
Self-illuminating and undistracted.

At the request of Puntsok Namgyal and Sönam Gyaltsen, this was written by Barway Dorje.

When Your Mind is Caught

When your mind is caught by recollection, it is seen.
Don't introduce the intellect's alterations. Leave it as it is.
If the doubt "Is this it or not?" arises, rest in that.
If the resolution "It is" arises, rest in it.
If the dissatisfied thought "It isn't" arises, let it go.
Whatever happens, be content with naked ordinariness.
Meditate on devotion for your guru and compassion for beings.

Dechen Barway Dorje wrote this to remind Karma Jangchup.

Appearances Are Lucidity-Emptiness

E MA HO. Appearances are lucidity-emptiness, the guru's body.
I pray to him with devotion.
Sounds are sound-emptiness, the guru's speech.
I pray to him with an outlook of purity.
Thoughts are awareness-emptiness, the guru's mind.
I pray to him with trusting faith.
The guru and my mind are indivisible.
I pray to him with certainty of this.

Distraction awakens awareness.
As soon as it's there it is fresh.
Don't alter or change it.
Stop everything and relax on the spot.

Let go of wanting to see, hope and fear, and thought.
Recollect diligence and give generously.
Composites are impermanent; cultivate revulsion.
Befriend benevolence and compassion.
Let go of ideas, plans, and talk.

Self-awareness is the ultimate wisdom.
Encounter it without seeing.
That will ensure perennial well-being.
This is advice for all Buddhists.

I, the blasé Buddhist Barway Dorje,
Have written these instructions that include
The dharmas of Mahamudra and the Great Perfection
In dharmic Palkyel Lhalung.

I Pray to My Root Gurus

I pray to my root gurus.
Bless me so that I recognize impermanence.
Bless me so that I remember death in my heart.

Do not take this ripened aggregate of form,
Composed of the four elements,
To be permanent. Remember death.
The changing of the four seasons is like a mirage.
There is nothing permanent. Keep this in mind.
Cultivate without distraction this self-aware, self-illuminating
  nature of mind.
You will greatly benefit now and later.
All you disciples who live here,
Diligently turn your minds inward.
Don't walk, sit, plan or do much.
Emphasize the implementation of what you know.
I have no other helpful advice to give.
May all you beloved disciples live long.
May you prosper and spontaneously accomplish dual good.
This was offered by Barway Dorje while visiting my homeland.

This was written by Barway Dorje for all my disciples, such as Kagyu Tulku, Urgyen Gyamtso, and Nyerpa Karma Özer. Virtue!

Uncommon Instruction on Generation and Completion

In order to fulfill the wishes of Gar Tulku of Lhana in Upper Ga, I composed this uncommon instruction on the points of generation and completion:

To all those who aspire to profound yoga:
In order to purify the appearances of this life,
Since your aggregates and elements are always deities,
Know them to be deities. Bring their clear appearance as
  such to the path.

From the first moment of waking,
Appearances are a pure realm, your body a deity's,
Your dwelling a palace, your companions gods and goddesses,
Speech mantra in nature, and thought the display of fresh
  self-awareness.
Vow never to stray from this.

The nature of an undistracted mind is empty.
A distracted mind is equally empty.
This mind-itself, whether distracted or not, is
  lucidity-emptiness.
Know that it is so unceasingly.

Food and drink are amrita. Actions are a magical dance.
Everything is always a boundless expanse of purity.
If you cultivate daytime appearances in this way,
At night the conceptual and nonconceptual clear lights of light
  and deep sleep
And thoughts in dreams will, like the daytime,
Be liberated upon arising, recognized, or will vanish into the
  expanse.
A yogi who cultivates this will be happy.

This is a description of qualities I lack.
However, I was unable to refuse the request of a great lama.
Therefore, amidst bouts of restless, endless sleep,
And overeating to the point where my kidneys were squished,
This cleric with a bad mouth and ears
Wrote this quickly, smiling to myself.
Through its virtue may the meditation of this great lama
  progress.
May he lead all connected to him to the realm of liberation.

Stainless Instantaneous Awareness

Your mind is stainless, instantaneous awareness.
Cultivate this through mere no-distraction.
Consider the causes of happiness and suffering.
Remember death. Meditate on devotion for your guru.
Always be benevolent toward everyone.
Help and serve everyone.
Dual benefit will be achieved automatically.
For the disciple Tenpa Dargyay,
This was written by Dechen Barway Dorje. Virtue!

If You Want Your Guru's Blessing

If you want your guru's blessing to enter your heart,
Pray continuously with fierce devotion.
The point of human life is holy dharma.
Don't be lazy in dharma; have fortitude.
Recognize your mind through mere attention.
During all activities, whether walking or seated,
Cultivate this. Great benefit will certainly occur.
Physical and verbal virtuous endeavors are the bases of merit.
Be disgusted by the business of samsara.
For Sönam Lhamo, Kalzang Lhamo, and all disciples,
These instructions were given by Barway Dorje. Virtue!

Dharmakaya, Your Own Benefit's Achieved

Dharmakaya, your own benefit's achieved.
Rupakaya, your benefit of others is unceasing.
I bow to my kind supreme guru.

Cultivate this fresh, natural mind-itself
Naturally, without fixation.
Abandon hope and fear of stillness and movement.
If the doubt "Is this it or not?" and the desire to see arise,
Rest in the nature of that for which they arise.
They will be self-liberated beyond the intellect.

Continually cultivate devotion for your guru
And attention unobscured by variations in behavior
Such as slow and fast or walking and sitting.
Great benefit will be accomplished.

Half your life has already been used up
By samsaric work and deeds.
It would be best if you let go of craving internally.
Guard samaya like your eyes.

Vows are the basis of dharma.
If they're broken, this life and the next are ruined.
If they're kept, you'll be happy and good now and in the end.
So keep them.

Your guru and your mind are inseparable,
Beyond distance or parting.
Always behave nobly.
Always be compassionate and benevolent toward others.

Since my disciple Könsam said,
"I require instruction and advice,"
This was written by Barway Dorje.

This Leisure and These Resources

This leisure and these resources are hard to get. Use them well.
Composites are impermanent. Be quickly diligent.
Causality is infallible. Believe it and make careful choices.
With renunciation, desire liberation from samsara.

Therefore, go for refuge and protection to the three jewels.
Purify wrongdoing, downfalls, and habits with four-powered confession.
Accumulate merit with actual and imaginary offerings.

Place all your hopes in your all-sufficient root guru.
Entrust to him your welfare in this life, the next, and between.
With unfluctuating devotion pray to him repeatedly,
Throughout the whole day and night.

Mix his mind and yours. Cultivate its nature.
That nature is awareness unpolluted by the three times' complexity.
Cultivate it without alteration, freshly, in arising-liberation.[19]
Don't add the opinionated intellect's changes.
Resolve everything within your mind alone.

Even if your view is high, do not disregard causality.
Even if your meditation is good, it is profound to cultivate aimlessness.
The best conduct is that soaked in attention.
If you eradicate doubt, that is the removal of impediments.
The more devotion you have, the more progress there will be.
If you've no hope and fear, you've accomplished the fruition, the trikaya.

This was written for the disciple Rinchen Gönpo
By the common mantrin Traktung Barway Dorje
As the lightning-like depiction of whatever arose,
In order to give absolute truth a chance to appear.
By its virtue, may any being that sees or hears this be benefited.

To My Guru

To my guru, who embodies all refuges—the three jewels—
I pray with anguished devotion.
Bless me so that I know the rarity of this precious free and
favored body,
And that I use it well.

Life is as impermanent as a candle in the wind.
May I become free from procrastination.
May I believe in the infallibility of causality,
The ripening of good and bad actions.

May I know that I have been fooled for innumerable lives
By the accomplishment of wealth and greatness in this world,
And by this endless business of samsara.
Bless me so that I give it up utterly in my mind.

May I always be protected by the three jewels.
May infractions, downfalls, wrongdoing, and obscurations be
purified in their own place.
May vast accumulations be completed through imaginary and
actual offerings.
May supreme bodhichitta be born in my continuum.

May my guru's blessing enter my heart.
May the empty enclosure appear as the rainbowlike deity body.
May I achieve freedom in the body vajra's channels and winds.
May the winds' coming and going be drawn into the avadhuti.

May the taming and training of the causal bodhichitta be
perfected.
May the pure and impure illusory bodies be realized to be
empty.
May I achieve freedom in the speech vajra's dreams.

May bliss and emptiness meet in the mind vajra's clear light.

May I realize the interval to be like an illusion.
May I achieve freedom on the path of ejection.
May the fruition, the four buddha bodies, be revealed.

From now on, for the rest of your life,
Pay no attention to the number of your recitations.
Walk along the border between generation and completion.

Don't meditate so you can say you've done it.
Turn your heart to your next life.
Don't peddle power and influence in this life
Or engage in litigious competition.

This life is short, momentary.
Don't grasp at solidity.
Apply your courage to holy dharma.
Cast your homeland behind you.

These Six Dharmas of Naro are the quintessence.
They are hard to find at any time.
This qualified holy guru
Is hard to find at any time.

If you focus on the essence of dharma
You'll automatically accomplish dual benefit.
Listen to my words and implement them.
May your pure wishes be fulfilled.

Instructions of Barway Dorje
For the monk Karma Rikdzin.

The Basis of Dharma

In order to establish the basis of dharma,
First consider the rarity of leisure and resources,
Death, impermanence, actions' results,
And the defects of samsara.

Then, uncommonly, take refuge,
Generate aspiration and implementation bodhichitta,
Purify obscurations, offer mandalas, and pray
To your guru with anguished devotion.

The main thing is your mind,
The root of all misery and joy, and of samsara and nirvana.
Although we take it to be a self,
Look for its origin, location, destination, going, and coming.

Examine where it is—outside or inside.
Has it color or shape?
Examine whether it is real or unreal.

It is emptiness, neither one nor many.
It is unoriginated, unfindable, and unceasing.
Whatever arises in your mind is fresh.

Look at what thinks.
Looking for it, you think, "Will I see it or not?"
Look at what feels hope and fear.
If there is nothing to look at,
Rest in that without thinking anything.

The view is exhaustion of the intellect.
Meditation is without intellectual engagement.
Rest in a state beyond the intellect.
Devotion and diligence are companions on the path.
Cultivate revulsion for samsaric doings.

If you meditate one-pointedly in that way,
You will gradually pass through all the stages of experience.
The wisdom of realization will arise effortlessly.
The fruition, perfect buddhahood, will quickly be attained.

For the use of the retreatant Lozang Tenpa, this was quickly written by Pal Traktung Gaway Yeshe Dechen Barway Dorje, a mantradharin of the end of time. Virtue!

OM AH HUM!

OM AH HUM!
Personification of the three times' buddhas,
Vidyadhara, you have appeared for the good of beings
From the vast expanse of Padmakara's compassion.
I pray to Dechen Barway Dorje.
Transfer your blessing and wisdom to my continuum.
Bless me so that I realize the unborn essence.

If our various thoughts are not embraced by awareness,
We waste our lives by wandering in bewilderment.
Even though there are frequent moments of distraction and forgetfulness,
As soon as awareness returns, cultivate it.
Don't intellectualize, alter, or fabricate.
By cultivating naturalness a great thing will be achieved.
In response to the request of a few male and female disciples,
This was immediately written by Barway Dorje. Virtue!

The Only Support

NAMO!
The only support for holy dharma
Is this free and favored human body.
Relying on your supreme guru's instructions,
Gather a vast accumulation of merit
By performing as much physical and verbal virtue as you can.

In order to tame the kleshas and thoughts in your mind,
Condense the path—generation and completion—into its essence.
Have the fortitude to bear sickness and even death.

Cultivate whatever arises with natural relaxation,
Leaving your mind in unaltered freshness.
Give up hope for bliss or clarity.
Do not fear obscurity or clarity's absence.
Without ambition or direction,
Rest within the nature of whatever arises.

The key is to drive the stake of devotion for your guru into your heart.
The river of blessings will definitely flow.
Always be free from vacillation.

If you want the warmth of experience,
You will have to be increasingly committed and diligent.
Be as courageous and forbearing as you can.
This is how the Great Repa attained liberation.[20]
If you want to emulate him, be brave.
Look up to good examples.
By keeping the samayas taught by your father guru,
Great things will be accomplished.

These words, a reminder for Sönam Chödrön,
Were spoken by the lazy old man Barway Dorje while relaxing.
They were written down by the miraculous fingers
Of the monk Ratna Shasadhara.
May this cause the supreme attainment!

In Response to the Request of My Disciple Ögya Dorje of Golok for a Prophecy

Lord of dharma, personification of kindness,
Truly indivisible from Guru Padma—
I pray to you from my heart
With an unaltered mind.

If poetic prophecies are incomprehensible
They do little good.
Beautiful little songs sadden us,
But few understand them.
Even if they are clear, words of advice
Are hard to follow in one's heart.

Holy dharma—the good path of sutra and tantra—is infallibly true.
If no one believes or implements it, however,
We waste our lives samsarically.
All our actions—walking, sitting, and conversation—are bewildered.
Don't turn this into a prophecy.

First, implement wholeheartedly
The words of holy dharma.
Second, have unfluctuating faith in and devotion for
Your root guru, the embodiment of all refuges.
Third, cultivate the inexpressible nature
Of this stainless, self-aware, self-illuminating mind.
Fourth, have little anger for your close and distant companions.
Fifth, have little craving for this world.

If you properly accomplish these five things
You'll achieve your aim in this life,
And I predict your final awakening.

Don't leave these words on the page; implement them.
Don't cast their meaning aside; apply them to yourself.

I, Barway Dorje, offer this
To my disciple Ögya Dorje,
An emanation of Kyiling Tekchok Dorje.

I offered this along with an image of Guru Rinpoche that I had consecrated myself, another image that was self-arisen during an amrita accomplishment, some of the accomplished amrita, a Wrathful Guru mantra doorguard, a breath-consecrated knot, and divine fabric. Virtue!

For Tseyang

The greatest of my secret companions, Tseyang, a dakini of family from the town of Tridu, requested a prophecy. This was my response:

KYE HO!
Listen, fortunate woman of good family!
Prophecies of the hidden future, good and bad,
Are given by victors omniscient of the three times.
I, an ordinary being, have no supercognition.
I dare not say anything at all.

However, based on profound scripture and reasoning,
I can predict the future results of right and wrong actions.
No prophecy beyond this is needed.

All who do evil will be born in bad migrations:
Through hatred and hurting others, in the eighteen hells;
Through desire and greed, as pretas;
And through apathy and distraction, as animals.
Learn the details of the ripened, concordant,
And dominant results from the books.

All who do good will go to higher states.
Those whose virtue is stained by the poisons
Of pride, jealousy, and desire will achieve
The states of gods, asuras, and humans respectively.
They will suffer downfall; battle; and birth, aging, sickness, and death.
They will experience alternate suffering and pleasure.

Those who fixatedly cultivate bliss, clarity, and no-thought
Will experience their respective results in the three realms.
Those whose minds are stuck on any of the four experiences of emptiness

Will be reborn in one of the four formless absorptions.

Those who meditate on external and internal selflessness
and interdependence
Will achieve the state of a shravaka or pratyekabuddha arhat.
Aspiration and implementation bodhichitta are the ground
of the mahayana.
The profound view is the system of our tradition.
Those who cultivate these will reach the authentic path.

The external and internal tantras correspond to individual
faculties.
Those who tame, purify, and master their bodies, speech, and
minds will achieve
The vidyadhara stages: ripened, life-mastery, mahamudra, and
spontaneously present.
Finally, they will accomplish the fruition, the two bodies.

The essence of the path is the accomplishment of virtue.
I predict that you will gradually accomplish it.

As for a prophecy of the immediate future:
It is natural that, having been born, you will age.
As for when you will die: that is unknown.
I prophesy that the interval will appear to you, as it does to all.

If you act dharmically, you'll profit now and later.
If you misbehave, you'll lose now and later.
In your family home, an enemy—hatred—awaits.
In society, an enemy—distraction—awaits.
Laziness and apathy could attack at any time.
Therefore, be diligent without procrastination.

Although you've now acquired a pure human body,
I prophesy that it will definitely die some day.
It is certain that friends can't protect us in the next life.

It is definite that enemies can't cast us into bad migrations.
Believe that the three jewels are infallible.
Ensure that you'll encounter your guru in your next life.

This aimlessly wandering beggar has no time
To write long, detailed instructions,
And rolling all points into one is more useful.
This song was written spontaneously as it occurred to me,
In repayment for kind assistance of body and speech.

This is a prophecy of holy liberation,
Of utter virtue in the end.

The woman Tseyang asked me for a prophecy of her future. In response I, the wanderer Traktung Gaway Yeshe Dechen Barway Dorje, wrote this in a moment. Virtue!

A Song to Dispel Sadness

When I was about to wander elsewhere, that same woman asked me for a song to dispel her sadness. This was my response:

Listen, young woman of family,
Faithful friend of my heart!
You have asked me, the yogin who wanders throughout
  the land,
To sing you a memento of our love,
Words to be kept in the heart,
Instructions to bring your mind to the dharma,
A song to ease your heart.
Maiden, I will sing and sing!

Among worldly people,
Fathers leave their sons advice,
Which few sons follow.
Worldly endeavors are meaningless.
Meditate on these instructions as advice for the future.
A stalwart son is his father's true son.
In the same way, if you can follow my advice, you will never
  be separate from me.
This is like a son taking after his father.

Mothers talk kindly to their daughters.
Few daughters listen.
Worldly talk is meaningless.
Make devotion your conversation.
Daughter of a loving mother,
If you have faith, you will never be separate from me.
This is like a daughter taking after her mother.

Masters instruct their servants.

Few servants do what they're told.
Worldly instructions are useless.
Meditate without respite on these, the essence of instructions.
If you practice dharma quickly, you are like the best of servants.
If you remember this, it is like a servant inseparable from her lord.

This wandering yogin loves faithful men and women.
He sings songs of profound dharmic instruction.
Few keep his words in mind.
There is no need for songs as entertainment.
The point of my songs is attention to causality.
Disciples, keep that in mind.
If you can pray with a devoted mind,
The father guru's compassion is without "near and far."
This is you taking after me.

The point of my words is this:
Think not only of this life, but of the next and beyond.
Reckon the results of right and wrong.
On the road that leads to either samsara or nirvana,
Don't choose wrongly between happiness and suffering.
Don't drown in the river of birth and death
Which feeds the ocean of samsara.
Get into the boat of practice!
Look toward the shore with eyes focused on liberation.
Bite your lip with the canines of fortitude.
With the strokes of generation and completion,
Holding fast to the oars of cause and result,
Row past the waters of distraction
To the island of liberation.
With faith and devotion, never forget
The kindness of the holy guru, your refuge and guide.
Girl who is fixed in my mind,

This is my response to your kindness.

Sometimes, when you are practicing,
You will remember your friend,
This wandering longhaired yogin.
Let this little song, sung to dispel sadness, be my substitute.
Let it be the support for your faith and a source of devotion.
Let my final words before I go
Be instructions that bring dharma to the path.
Let them serve as an aspiration to meet you often
And as a portent of our meeting soon.

This was written by the wanderer Traktung Barway Dorje for a young woman who possesses genuine devotion. Virtue!

Advice and Instruction

In reply to her further request for a song of advice and instruction, this was my response:

Kye ho!
Listen, fortunate one!
First, you were born in a good family.
Your birth is not inferior; you were born as a dakini.
But then you were cast into the crowd of the worldly,
And were somewhat corrupted by vulgar bewilderment.
You were contaminated by the breath of demonic friends.
However, your actions were good; you are devoted to dharma.
You met a holy, qualified guru.
You tasted the amrita of instruction.
You are fortunate to have met me.

This yogin isn't saying this to praise himself.
I met the lord guru in my youth.
I then studied as well as I could.
Finally, I devoted myself to practice,
Meditating on profound generation and completion.
The signs of the path of channels, winds, and drops arose.
I bear the signs of a hero of authentic family,
Connection with whom is meaningful.
That is why meeting me has been the timely awakening
Of a karmic connection from past lives,
Maintained by good aspirations.

After we made a physical connection,
You never saw me as a lover, but as a guru.
You were definitely born with the mahayana disposition.

After we began to converse,

You never saw it as talk, but as instruction.
You are definitely a vessel for profound dharma.

When we cultivated our skill in bliss-emptiness,
Your faith and affection blazed like fire.
It is certain that our connection is due to past karma.

Now, we shall not meet for a while.
You have said, "I require instruction!"
Those words, spoken by you in love, have moved me.
I'll summarize the essential points of practice.

Listen, qualified one of authentic family,
Young woman linked to me by our hearts,
Supreme companion in the achievement of great bliss!

Having trained your being through the common preliminaries,
Accumulate and purify through the uncommon ones.
Always meditate on your body as that of the deity
And on all appearances as the deity's form.
That will purify physical wrongs and veils,
And bring about the arising of undifferentiated pure appearances.

Meditate on all utterance of speech as the sound of mantra.
That will purify verbal wrongs and veils,
And bring about the natural accomplishment of the three roots.

Look at your mind, self-awareness.
Has it substance, color, shape, or characteristic?
If not, look to see where it is—inside or outside.
If you don't find it, look to see if it is the one who's looking.
If it is, look at what is searching.
If it isn't, look at what is aware.
Look to see if experience and thought are two.
If there are no looked-at and looker,

That is what is called the "mind's empty nature."

Experience doesn't stop.
Look to see where thoughts first arise;
Then where they remain, come, and go;
And finally, where they end and are destroyed.
Looking, you don't see anything.
Like a water-moon or a mirror's reflection,
Appearance-emptiness and clarity-emptiness are each indivisible.
This has been the mind's nature from the beginning.
Looking at it now, you resolve that it has.
Then, when you apply this in meditation,
You see it just by thinking, "I shall look at my mind."
If there is no directed focus, let go in that.
There is nothing to see; don't search for something.
There being nothing to be meditated on is itself the absolute truth.
Don't engage in the intellect's spying.
The experience of nothing to be done, beyond the intellect, is authentic.
Whatever occurs, rest in that state.
Take the absence of good and bad on the path.
Being without acceptance and rejection is the conduct,
Without any hope or fear, stopping or creating.
The ordinary, unaltered mind is revealed.
That is the beginning of the gradual result.

In support of this, for correction and enhancement,
Don't allow generation and completion, the boat to liberation,
To develop the leak of procrastination.
Apply the sealant that is the recollection of there being no leisure.
Don't lose the oars of diligence, which maintain
The path's speed, in the waves of attachment.
Give rise to exertion through the recollection of death.

With heartfelt devotion, entrust yourself utterly
To the guru, the undeceiving captain,
And be free of capriciousness.
While still not liberated from samsara's ocean,
Fear the crocodiles of bad karma.
Beware the mischief of relatives—the fish and beavers.
Through birth, the poisonous belly of the frog opens wide.
Sickness is a fish thrashing about on hot sand.
Aging is a snake slithering through a valley.
The taste of death is unavoidable.
The horns of death, the water buffalo, are sharp.
So don't be attached to samsara.
It's time to reach the dry land of liberation.
Therefore be diligent without distraction.

As well, whatever signs you experience,
Don't get excited; that's a great mara.
Whatever agitation and suffering arise,
They are just temporary side effects; look at their nature.
Whatever joy and pleasure arise,
Regard them as the guru's kindness.
That will cause your merit to increase and be inexhaustible.
Whatever undesired misery arises,
Believe it to be past karma.
That will sweep away wrongs and downfalls.
Never carelessly denigrate
Any aspect of the three jewels.
Don't get lost in negativity and antipathy.
Meditate on impartial compassion
For our parents, all beings of the three realms.
Dedicate your virtue to beings.

If you practice all of this, not abandoning it,
The roots of dharma are complete.
The essence of meditation is complete.

This has been my experience.
These are my instructions to you.
They are undeceiving, young one.
Liberation of your mind is certain, one of authentic family.

These words were written at the request
Of my dear friend with the signs of a dakini,
Named Tsering,
By a yogin crowned with a topknot,
Given by matrikas and dakinis of the expanse the name
Pal Traktung Barway Dorje,
At the dharma camp of Tashi Ling,
In one session break.
I dedicate all virtue to beings.
May they attain omniscient buddhahood.

Unafraid of Death

My disciple from Ojong, Norgyay, requested instructions that would make him unafraid of death. In response, I wrote this:

NAMO AMITABHAYE
To the protector Amitabha,
Indivisible from my root guru,
I pray with unbearable devotion.

As soon as recollection arises in your mind,
Rest in it without alteration,
Free of viewer and viewed.
Even if your mind moves, cultivate its nature.
If torpor arises, increase your exertion.
If you recognize whatever thoughts occur
In spite of their being good or bad,
They are beyond adoption and rejection.

Always contemplate impermanence and revulsion.
Always imagine your guru above your head.
Turn your mind to him and mix it with his.

At death, offer your wealth as a mandala.
Let go of craving for possessions and loved ones.
Pain and suffering are your mind.
Cultivate its nature one-pointedly without distraction.

In the center of your empty-clear body is the avadhuti.
It is hollow, white outside, and red inside.
Its top widens; its bottom is sealed.
Within it, at your heart, on a moon, is your consciousness,
A white sphere the size of a pea.
Shoot it repeatedly into your guru's heart.
If you can, repeat supplications and HIK.

If not, the meditation is enough.

Then, when appearance, increase, and attainment
Arise as whiteness, redness, and blackness,
No matter what happens, cultivate its nature.
No matter what appears, look at your own nature.
If you become bewildered, think of Sukhavati.
Think of suffering as purification.

During the clear appearance of the first clear light,
Cultivate your own nature; reunite mother and child.
When the clear light appears as deities' bodies in the interval of dharmata,
Give rise to devotion; they are your own appearance as deities.

If you experience bewilderment in the interval of becoming,
Meditate on revulsion for this world.
To the west is a pure realm.
Enter, with miraculous power,
The presence of your guru, Amitabha.
You'll be miraculously born in a lotus
And become the equal of all bodhisattvas.
You'll receive assurance and prophecy.
Think of all this and you'll certainly be born there.

For my disciple Norgyay,
This was written by Barway Dorje.
May it lead all who encounter it
To the realm of Sukhavati.

Instructions Given to Old Lama Nyuwa at Kyodrak

KYE HO! Yogins, when you die,
Resolve to offer your body and all you own
To your guru and the three jewels.
Know wrongdoing to be without essence, empty.
Joyously recollect virtue's benefits.
Imagine your guru always above your head.
Cultivate the nature of your mind indivisible from your guru.

This interval between birth and death is like a dream.
Don't suffer through fear of death, yogins.
Meet the dharmakaya in the reunion of the mother and child clear lights.
Meet the sambhogakaya deities during the interval of dharmata.
Purify the illusory body with the clear light during the interval of becoming.
Dispatch nirmanakayas for beings' good during the interval of the birthplace.
They are all dharmata, empty in nature.
Look at the spectacle of their unlimited, illusory display.

While undergoing sickness, pain, fluctuating lucidity and dullness,
And the three stages of death—appearance, increase, and attainment—
There is nothing to do but cultivate awareness's self-recognition.
Give up any idea that there is anything better than that to do or think about.
There is nothing at all other than cultivating just this mind-itself.

Old lama, your uncertainty and question have been answered
By this verbose old mantrin in this introduction.
It was written down by Dulwa as I spoke.
May you reach the city of the clear light, the dharmakaya.

The Experiences and Realizations of Padma Tsewang

The Lord Vidyadhara's eldest son, Padma Tsewang Dechen Chokdrup, was praised by the Terchen and Dharmaraja Urgyen Chokgyur Dechen Lingpa and other holy beings as the rebirth of Prince Lharjay. In this song, Padma Tsewang offered his experiences and realizations:

NAMO GURU!
Single lord, whose deeds are beyond measure,
First, you generated this illusory body of mine.
Then you supported me with material resources.
Ultimately, you showed me the ordinary essence.
To my only father of such kindness,
I offer this spontaneous song of experience
Of the path of generation and completion.

This body is the great mandala of the wisdom of great bliss.
In the cities of the channels, chakras, and the avadhuti,
I have seen the bodies of deities and the garlands of syllables.
The vajra repetition, speech like an echo,
Is mantric sound without abiding, coming, or going.
I understand its unceasing vibration of pure speech
To be the expanse of the ultimate vajra sound.
My mind's thoughts, the upsurge of dharmakaya,
Are beyond removal, addition, and craving.
Whatever appears is the great play of wisdom.
I understand whatever arises to be great bliss beyond action.

When I view this mind that views objects,
The viewer is lost in space.
Awareness-emptiness without center or limit arises.
I have realized that meditation and subsequent attainment are
beyond alternation.
When I practice meditation,

Fixation on the act of meditation dissolves in space.
The nature is unceasing.
I understand spontaneously present great openness.
When I practice the conduct,
Fixation on the act of conduct is lost in space.
There is no relinquishment or remedy needed no matter what arises.
I understand this to be the wisdom of Samantabhadra.
I look forward to wandering in the illusory city of the bardo.
My mind, no-self, is without the root of bewilderment.
My body will appear clearly as the real deity.
I want to test my skill in emanation and transformation.

I know that all these external appearances are the play of mind.
I have realized that this internal awareness is unchanging.
I understand that there is no border between meditation and subsequent attainment.
My mind's six groups arise without relinquishment or acceptance.
There is nothing in all of samsara and nirvana to be accepted or rejected.
In the state free of engagement in imputation
There is nothing to do. I remain without altering the nature.
I understand that whatever arises is beyond being stopped or created.

I have cast aside the deceptive dharmas of the indicative meaning.
I have taken the definitive meaning as my outlook.
Having torn apart the net of dualistic appearances,
I understand that appearances and mind are not two.
Intoxicated by the liquor of the path of bliss-emptiness,
I have untied the knots of hope and fear.
Having built the fortress of no-distraction,
I have destroyed the shack of thought.
Having cultivated the practice of no fixation,

The craving of fixation has vanished.
Having the meaning of nothing-to-do in mind,
The bonds of imputation have been cut in resolution.

Through the kindness of my glorious guru and deities,
Delight has been born in my heart.
In the varied appearances of meditation and dreams
I have received introduction through symbols and words.
While offering a feast at Pomne,
From within the rocks up there
Appeared a dancing blue yogin,
Adorned by jewels and leaves,
Holding a skullcup of amrita.
He said to me, "Hey! Great yogin! Drink this!"
He gave it to me and I drank it, I dreamed.
In a pleasant meadow at Tsukpu
While in virtuous retreat I saw
The glorious sixth buddha, Mahavajradhara,[21]
Sky-blue and blazing with marks and signs,
Wearing the sambhogakaya attire,
As vivid as a rainbow in the sky.
An inexpressible experience arose.
Bliss and emptiness became inseparable in my mind.
Henceforward, I knew how to cultivate wind-mind.
Sometimes agitation and sometimes vague,
Mistlike experiences have continued to arise, but really
Whatever thoughts of pleasure and pain occur,
I have no one else to tell them to but you, father.
Have I achieved practice that can withstand death, or not?
Please continue to keep me in your heart!

In response, his father—the noble guru Vajradhara—wrote:

Hey! Listen, my disciple,
My son, produced by the six elements of my body,

Whom I love more than my eyes and heart,
From early childhood until now
I have supported you in the mundane way with food and clothing.
I have filled your ears with the dharma of the New and Old traditions.
I have advised you on what's good and what's bad to do with your mind.
Let that be your inheritance.
Don't waste it; practice it.

Now you have asked me about your signs of warmth.
I think that your recognition of all dharmas as mind
Is the final resolution of the view.
About the appearance of your external body as a deity,
The spectacles you have seen as the nature of the internal channels and winds,
The mastery you have gained of nondual wind-mind,
And your eradication of the dichotomy between meditating and not—
I think you have mastered the clear light.
In relaxed, natural nothing-to-do,
There is no conduct and no conductor.
There is no hope for peace, nirvana,
And no need to fear existence, rebirth in samsara.
Really, once you are liberated from the net of hope and fear,
You have achieved the actual result.
When you master emanation and transformation in the waking state
You can perform these at will while asleep and dreaming.
You see pure and impure appearances as entertainment.
Your mastery of the illusory body is clear.
Once you can enter and withdraw from the clear light in dreams
And whatever you do does not deviate from awareness-emptiness,

You have accomplished your own benefit.

Son, this talk of yours is good, not bad,
For you have now accomplished your permanent well-being.
The hopes of your old father are fulfilled.

Then, that holy son offered his father his realization of the appearance of the clear light:

Father, guru of threefold kindness,
Emanation and transformation of daytime appearances
And entering and leaving the clear light of sleep are still
  not easy.
Although I think I grasp most dreams with awareness,
I am still intimidated by unpleasant experiences.
I beg of you further instruction about this.

In response, his lord father replied:

Listen, child of my family:
To test the path in dreams,
View these daytime appearances as sleep and dreams.
To cultivate this habit,
Meditate on dreams and the illusory body combined.
To transform and emanate pure and impure bodies,
Imagine the realms of the ten directions.
Greet the teachers in those realms.
Request empowerment and prophecy.
Receive dharma and return home.
Imagine this repeatedly.
Once trained in this there will be no difficulty
In emanation or transformation in dreams.

Now, about unpleasant experiences
And entering and leaving the clear light:
Moving from dreams to the clear light and back
Is a practice of father tantra.
One arises from the clear light into a dream,
Then reenters the clear light.
However, there may be instability of recognition.
Your attention may be distracted by thoughts.
Really, the main factor is how used to it you are.
This is the instruction of the tantras.
The qualities come from habituation.
There is no doubt they'll arise over time.

The first step is to recognize dreams as dreams.
Then the thought of recognizing the dream must be recognized.
That is the clear light within dreams.
Please keep all this in mind.

The Songs of Padma Trime Loden

The lord of yogins, Padma Trime Loden, was the greatest of the lord guru's dharma disciples. For a garland of many lives, such as when Trime Loden was Lharje Rokchen and when he was Repa Shiwaö, he had had an uncommonly close relationship with his guru. He offered him this euphonic vajra song:

Indivisible embodiment of all victors, Mahavajradhara,
Düdül Lingpa, conqueror of adversity and darkness,
You who abide vividly in the lotus of my heart—
I offer you the stamens of my undivided faith.

This pure support with eighteen freedoms and resources,
This precious human body, has not been wasted.
In reliance on a holy spiritual friend, that excellent condition,
  I received the best method,
The essence of holy dharma, the profound and secret sutras
  and tantras.
I examined these appearances of bewilderment
In both aspect and ultimate nature.
No matter what emerged from the unbewildered ground,
The old man of wisdom within my mind,
I lay down without care in my own bed, the ground.
I came to know the nature of all the good and bad I'd done.
Without complacence due to learning, I applied the
  instructions;
I remained in my seat and analyzed without hope or fear.
In meditation beyond doing, even placement and subsequent
  attainment mixed.
My lack of hesitation in spontaneously writing this song
  of experience
Is due to your kindness, noble one.

The view is the unity of appearance-emptiness beyond doer and deed.
Meditation is nonconceptual luminosity, an unwavering expanse.
Within it, conduct is yogic discipline beyond acceptance and rejection.
Having cast aside this ruinous fixation on a self,
I am automatically victorious over birth and death.
Appearances have become unobstructing, the magical illusion of relative truth.
Allowing whatever appears as an external object to liberate itself,
Bewildered thoughts don't truly exist and are empty of themselves.
Mountains and rocks don't stand up; they are transparent and penetrable.

The experience of the profound secret of the dakinis, the connate bliss of melting,
I have cultivated to perfection. Through its illusory interdependence
I do not crave the pleasure of bewildered appearances; I revel in great bliss.
The pure nature of the elements and winds is a body of light.
It is the wisdom display of dharmadhatu, great bliss.
I have experienced the full, undefiled four joys.

Although the word *dharmakaya* is so renowned,
It refers to nothing more than this very stainless mind.
Samsara and nirvana are self-liberated and inseparable! A LA LA!

In that way, my lord, your disciple Padmamati
Presents his experience as a spontaneous song of offering.
Jampal Dorje Tritsun, undisputed great treasure-revealer,
Dechen Barway Dorje, I offer this to you.
I request further instruction in the view.

In response his guru, Mahavajradhara, exhibited great joy and sang the following vajra song of ultimate experience:

A LA LA HO indeed!
Your supreme supports for the ultimate achievement of holy dharma,
Your precious leisure and resources, have not gone to waste.
Your experience of your own benefit is excellent.
Such talk as this between guru and disciple is a joy!

There are no objects of appearance beyond the mind.
There is no mind apart from appearances.
Appearances and mind, objects and subject, are not two things.
Rest freely and naturally in that state.

When the naughty child of bewildered thought appears through habit,
Let him enter natural freedom. Don't reject or try to change him.
Relax at ease, free from delight at stillness and distress at movement.
Drink the breast milk of no-elaboration, the three gates of liberation.
Sleep in the clear light beyond increase and decrease.

These appearances, virtue and evil, are like the dreams of a magician.
Karmic appearances, like designs in water, are invisible to the blind.
Like magical illusions, without fixation, merit is undefiled.
Dedicate it to unreal beings, like a crowd seen in a dream.

The bright cloud of virtue, riding the sunrays of aspiration,
Dissolves into the sky of the dharmadhatu, without focus and undefiled.

The dark cloud of wrongdoing is driven by the wind of self-fixation.
It gathers above the all-basis as a blizzard of suffering.

Light and dark karmic appearances
Are the display of dharmata as interdependence.
Hope for virtue and happiness is a fetter of gold or silver.
Fear of wrongdoing and suffering is a battle in a dream.
It is nonexistent in its nature, a display unborn from the beginning.

The resolution of the essencelessness of appearances
Is the external breakthrough of objects.
The resolution that thoughts are unborn from the beginning
Is the internal breakthrough of oneself.
Resting freely in the nonduality of subject and object
Is the secret breakthrough.
Unaltered self-awareness, free of hope and fear, is self-illuminating.

Appearances cannot stand alone.
They are the conditional appearances of the six groups.
Nonexistent from the beginning,
External appearances are unborn.

The past mind is without origin, ground, or root.
The present mind is awareness in which seen and seer are indivisible.
The future mind is uncertain, free of cessation.
As the three times' complexity is nonexistent,
Mind is without birth or limitation.

It is the bad habit of thought that keeps one's mind from knowing itself.
We are foolish and infantile when we look outside for the fault within.

Mistaking our faults as others' casts us into the five poisons' abyss.
Whoever wants "good" is bloated by doubt.
Their ceaseless search for delicious meat is spoiled by the salt of reification.

A rash view of emptiness is grasping the supreme medicine with unquenchable desire.
This old man need do nothing about stillness or movement.
Hope and fear lie dormant like a dog sniffing in the dark.
There is nothing to search for. Search for the searcher.
Since there is nothing to do, I've stopped doing anything.
There is nothing to think about. Everything is beyond the intellect.

You've understood and examined dharma.
You cultivate devotion, generation, and completion ceaselessly.
Great lord of yogins, you are one-pointedly diligent.
In order to please you and gratify your insistent demand,
I, Barway Dorje, have written whatever words appeared to me.
A LA LA HO! For the benefit of all disciples newly entering the path,
This little song of important points of experience
Is offered to you all. May you laugh with white smiles of pleasure!

Again, his holy disciple offered a song expressing his certainty:

A LA LA! I bow to the feet of the noble lord Jvala Vajra!
Your kindness in bestowing such instructions is beyond recompense.
You are the dramatic display of Samantabhadra Mahavajradhara
As the sambhogakaya, the all-seeing Manjushri;

His display, Manjushrimitra;
And the exhibition of his mind, Düdül Lingpa.
Vidyadhara Dechen Barway Dorje, hear me!

I'm a fool like an old bull, with only three concerns.[22]
I've never for an instant sought fame or position in this life.
Through the supreme means—the accumulation of vast merit —
And the knowledge that is wisdom,
My "self" has appeared as the thoughtless all-basis consciousness.
The all-basis' nature is unborn, thoughtless, and lucid.

Without distraction, looker or looked-at, I've cut right through.
The self-arisen, lucid-empty, complexity-free nature has recognized itself.
By looking at arising thoughts in lucidity-emptiness without fixation,
The six consciousnesses relax. Subject and object are unborn.

In the great city of all things like dreams or illusions,
Devotion, emptiness, and compassion arise of themselves.
The unborn nature has been, from the beginning, beyond apprehension,
Spontaneously ubiquitous, universal.

In the mansion of primordially pure, self-illuminating, perfect clear light;
In the expanse of the non-abiding, unrestricted, pure three aspects;
In the ultimate, indestructible, rootless, self-illumination,
Pure dharmata dissolved into the space of the clear light.

This little song of my experience of unborn, primordial purity's light
Is offered to the feet of the noble lord Shepa Dorje.

The guru replied:

The unborn wisdom of primordial purity is not existent.
It is not nonexistent.
It is beyond the intellect,
Like the expanse of space.

Then, the guru sang this song:

A HO! Trime Loden, holy son of my heart,
The nature of all dharmas is the absence of origination.
You have experienced seeing this directly,
And have relinquished active effort in the transcendence of activity.
You've exposed the lie of the superimposition of samsara, nirvana, birth, and death.
This is the ultimate profound wisdom of Samantabhadra and Vajradhara.
Unceasing naturalness is the primordially pure nature.
Unaltered spontaneous perfection is beyond change and the changed.
Therefore, in the expanse of the dharmakaya, all appearances are pure.
In the all-pervasive, undifferentiated exhaustion of intellect and dharmas,
Great yogin, rest easy and aimlessly.

The Song of Karma Ngedön Nyingpo

This song was offered by Karma Ngedön Nyingpo, a tulku of Kyodrak:

Single father, kind lord, all refuges embodied,
I have meditated through imagination on the authentic meaning.
I have kept dharma, twofold selflessness, in my heart.
I have entered the passage of the path, the two stages.
I wonder if I haven't gained irreversible confidence
In the great secret, the vehicle of fruition.
I know that all this is through your kindness, lord.
From now until awakening,
Never stop gazing upon me with great love.
Please ripen me with the amrita of your speech.

In reply, the lord Barway Dorje wrote:

My son, you intelligent, supreme nirmanakaya!
Your body is nothing more than an aggregate to which you cling.
Analyze its parts, down to subtle particles.
When analyzed, it is seen to be empty.
Your awareness is emptiness itself.
Its display is unreal appearances.
Meditate on them as the rainbowlike body of a deity.
Be without great fixation on reality.
Cultivate the nature of self illuminating self-awareness.
I offer this to the eyes of this supreme nirmanakaya.
Please be persistent and courageous in meditation.

The Song of Kagyu Tashi

I, Kagyu Tashi, am also among the ranks of this lord's disciples. When I was in my twenty-third year, I offered him this song describing my ascertainment of the nature:[23]

NAMO GURU VAJRADHARAYE!
Father, noble lord, buddha, Vajradhara,
Glorious Mipam Chökyi Senge:
Until I reach the heart of awakening,
Care for me in all my lives.

I've now acquired precious leisure and resources.
I enjoy the amrita of definitively secret dharma.
Although I wish to emulate holy beings,
My continuum is misled by kleshas and bewildered thought.

My previous lives were wasted in distraction.
I now see the suffering of birth and death.
I feel the frustration of someone on a long journey.
Father, Vajradhara, hold me in your compassion.

In the year of the Earth Ox,
In the hermitage of accomplishment at Kyijam,
With one word you separated samsara and nirvana.
You introduced me to self-awareness, the dharmakaya.

I repeatedly remind myself of this,
But I'm frequently misled by distracting thoughts.
Consequently, my experience and realization
Are like the children of the childless.

Still, I've resolved that there's no buddha
To be found outside my mind.
Whatever good and bad thoughts arise in my mind,

I am never without recollecting awareness.
It is beyond intentional meditation.
I can't describe it as "this" or "that."
I wonder if the terms "distracted" and "undistracted"
Don't simply refer to a mind with or without recollection.

I pray that you grant me a letter!

I've heard that while meditating on the ground, the nature of
things,
There are a few critical mistakes one might make.
I therefore request further guidance on means
Of correction and progress.

In response to my request, the lord did bestow a reply. This was the honey that emerged from the lotus petals of his lips:

My son, blessed by the Kagyu,
Listen to me for a moment.

The blessings of dharma—
Virtue in the beginning, middle, and end—
Are unimpaired, child of my heart.
How could you not be breast-fed by the ultimate lineage?

The three channels of your body are cities of dakinis.
The milk of their blessings, experience of the ultimate,
Will nourish you as you grow, worthy child.
Its quintessential power will reach your heart.
May you follow in the footsteps of our Kagyu forefathers.

Even in the present depths of fivefold degeneration,
Supported by a body with the flawless six elements
You've gone forth to the Victor's doctrine.
You've done your best to maintain the three trainings.

Through dual benevolence in thought and deed,
You've never harmed yourself or others.
I think the authorized seals are complete in you.[24]

If the firewood of kleshas is not gathered,
The great fire of wisdom will not blaze.
Through great secret means do your best to cultivate
all appearances,
Sounds, and awareness as the three vajras.
That gives a human life meaning.

Bring all good and bad thoughts and cognition to the path
With the means of indivisible awareness-emptiness.

The clouds, mist, and fog that emerge
In the empty expanse of the sky
Are the display of the sky as their ground.
If all the experiences of pleasure and pain
That occur in the mind—the great expanse of thatness—
Are known to be groundless, it is understanding.
If they are realized to be rootless, it is realization.

You are earnestly applying, through awareness,
This profound introduction to the nature.
There is no danger of error in this.
The ground, path, and fruition are inseparable.
All the qualities of the path arise at once.
Don't get caught in the net of hope and fear.

In the sky of the view beyond the intellect
Soar like a great garuda through the meditation of
awareness-emptiness.
Fly over the abysses of samsara and nirvana.
Engage in spontaneous and unlimited conduct.
The two aims will be spontaneously accomplished.

The Songs of Tsering Gönpo

Lama Tsering Gönpo, a disciple of this lord who was diligent in accomplishment, offered this song describing the indications that arose when he performed the approach and accomplishment of the White Khechari of Great Bliss:

E MA! When I was in the mountain fastness of Dalung,
Accomplishing the profound path—
The supreme instructions of the dakini
Through which one can reach the city of the dakinis
By means of sindhura, without relinquishing this ripened body—
These were my visions, experiences, and dreams:

One night I entered a palace I'd never seen before.
It was decorated by many victory banners and flags.
One night I dreamt that a wondrous boy
Spun a white parasol over my head, saying,
"I have no time to spin it. You spin it now."

One night I dreamt that many vultures flew from the west.
They landed and turned into indescribably beautiful maidens.
One among them was dark blue in color. I embraced her
And immediately reached the pure celestial realm.

One night I dreamt of a great gathering of women.
In union with their leader,
I asked her to take me to the celestial realm.
She said, "Don't be in a hurry. You'll go there later."

One night I dreamt that I went up the mountain.
The sun was rising and the flowers were colorful.
A large white bird was flying in the sky.
She said, "You're bewildered and very silly!
Don't you recognize me?

I'm inseparable from this whole expanse!
If you can, go to Uddiyana!"

One night I dreamt that I was a sixteen-year-old boy,
Wearing clothes of white silk and radiating light.
One night I dreamt that seated on my sindhura
Were Shakyamuni and Amitabha, both smiling.
Gazing upon me, they disappeared like rainbows.

One day, during a daytime session,
Dhateshvari, white, a cubit in size,
Actually appeared from the sky
And dissolved into the sindhura before me.

One evening, in the rays of an offering lamp
I saw gathered rainbow clouds.
Red light like lightning shot from them
And dissolved into the sindhura.

Also, amidst rainbow rays and vajra chains,
I saw a white buddha in sambhogakaya dress,
His hands touching the earth and at rest.
He dissolved into me.

Once, many meditation deities actually appeared
And dissolved into me and the supports.
In one experience at dawn I entered a palace
And saw many deities presided over by Samantabhadra.

He said, "All beings connected to you as friends or enemies
Will eventually be born in the realm Piled Lotuses."
Then he dissolved into space like a wispy cloud.

At dawn of the day I did an enriching fire offering,
I dreamt that I stood on the roof of a vast palace.
The sky was filled with wish-fulfilling jewels.

I reached out and grabbed two of them.

These word-strings describing my experiences
Are offered to my lord father's ears.
I pray that you grant me a vajra song
Telling me whether all this is good or bad.

In response, the noble lord, the precious guru, wrote this song about the meaning of dreams:

Now listen, you yogin!
You've been with me for a long time,
So your request is stuck in my heart.
I'll answer it.

All the appearances of existence are bewilderment.
Groundless bewilderment is called "double bewilderment."
Sometimes it is the trickery of gods and demons.
This causes agitated thoughts of good and bad.
Sometimes it is merely due to past habits.
This intensifies fixation on appearances.

When the karmic winds of consciousness
Enter the dakinis' cities in your body's channels,
Various appearances of pleasure and suffering arise.

Your dreams indicate the following:
Clear appearance of your body as a deity in meditation,
Signs of warmth in your verbal recitation,
And your ascertainment of the authentic meaning.

First, the six dreams you described
Are certain signs of accomplishment in this life.
They represent all six perfections.
The six visions and experiences you described

Are signs of warmth in approach, accomplishment, and activity.

The white buddha you saw was Vairochana,
The supreme lord of family.
The other signs are certain indications
Of your accomplishment of the supreme substance.

The sounds and prophecies you heard are certain,
But don't get lost in pride.
The dream on the day of the fire offering
Indicates your quick accomplishment of that activity.

If you do this twice or thrice without vacillation,
You'll definitely accomplish your aim, son of your father.
Don't let your mind become busy.
Please cultivate the experience of inactivity.
Don't ask others; decide for yourself.
Son, your wishes will be accomplished.

When he was close to the end of his retreat, that same disciple offered the following song about a vision combining meditation experience and dreams:

Single, wondrous, excellent lord,
Peerless father, beings' protector:

One night, in thought mixed with dreams,
I found myself facing west, near a vast valley,
On the peak of a grass-covered mountain resplendent with
flowers.

Within the clear appearance of the connate mother,
I looked upon all before me as a spectacle.
The sun and moon shone in the midst of the sky,
Surrounded by a multitude of stars.

There were small clouds and tentlike rainbows.
A gentle, honeyed rain fell as softly as dew.
The ground below was dazzling with flowers.
Amidst five-colored light were you, noble lord.

Your body was visible. You rode a steed
Whose four hoofs were supported
By the dakinis of the four families.
The mother, the white dakini, led your mount.
All of you floated a cubit above the ground.
I saw you passing into the sky.

I thought, "He is going to the celestial realm!"
At the moment that thought arose,
You and your retinue turned to look at me.
I heard the five mother dakinis
Sing this song with one voice:

"Son, listen! This, our only brother,
Has repeatedly, for seventeen lives,
Given you beings the greatest help.
Since he has now achieved the perfect vajra body,
He is going to the celestial realm of Uddiyana.
He will take the form of a heruka,
And has been asked to lead the feasts of the dakinis.
This profound dharma, the dakinis' hearts' blood,
Is better than a hundred thousand sadhanas of mother tantra.
Practice it, and the extent of its blessings will be clear.
Its great benefit will slowly spread.
All connected, practice it!
These are our final words; repeat them to everyone!"

I dreamt that after singing that, they led you to the west.
I've not forgotten this; it is clear in my mind.
Not really understanding its meaning, I left it alone.
I'm unsure whether it's a good or bad omen.

Since it's become a cause of uncertainty,
Please, omniscient guru, reveal to me
Its meaning, good or bad.

The lord replied:

Son, you are so affectionate to me,
Diligent, and devoted!

What a spectacular dream!
The beautiful realm with the mountain in its center
Is a sign that you possess samadhi.
This is a sign of your qualities, yogin!

The shining of the sun and moon high in the sky
Is a sign that you will become a peerless lineage holder.
The surrounding stars filling the sky
Are a sign that you will have many disciples.

The white clouds and tent of rainbows
Are signs that the dakinis will gather around all of you.
The gentle rainfall from the sky is a sign
That you will moisten beings' continuums with profound
dharma.

The dazzling flowers on the ground
Are a sign that the seedling of awakening will ripen.
These are signs of the benefit of this holy dharma.

This fellow appearing amidst fivefold light
Is a sign of manifest wisdom.
The horse is the four feet of miracle.[25]

Being held by the dakinis represents the factors of awakening.
Passing through space represents the dharmadhatu.

These are signs of this old man's qualities.

I've been cared for by dakinis since childhood.
Although I've been incapable of diligent practice,
External and internal signs of warmth have appeared
spontaneously.
My view of the nature is authentic.
I think that, no matter what, I'm headed for the dakinis' city.

All of us turning to face you, my son,
At the moment your mind called to us
Is a sign that your samaya is without deception.
The song they sang with one voice
Is a certain prophecy of the future.

Their instruction to repeat this to all disciples
Means that whoever practices this sadhana for a month
Will give birth to certainty within.

I'm old and unafraid of death,
But my work is not quite done.
There's a slight indication here of the dakinis' reception.[26]
It would be best if you disciples performed an Abiding
Ceremony.

Gurus bestow the inheritance of dharmic blessings.
Disciples perform the service of devotion.
In the end, no matter what, they are perfected as one group.

Don't have great craving for this life.
Be without fixation toward anything.
Cultivate the pure appearance of objects.
View all companions as Vajrayogini.

View all food as the five meats and amritas.
Behave according to the dakinis' secret words.

Complete the accomplishment and application.
Then travel, not remaining in one place.

Abandon association beyond mere acquaintance.
Wander through markets and crowds.
Once you've the confidence of no hope or fear
And cut through all craving for places and regions,
You'll be accomplished without fail, my son.

Although I don't possess unobstructed wisdom,
The five eyes, or the supercognitions,
I've explained the interdependence of your dream
In my own words and without secrecy.
Disciples, keep all this in mind!

The Songs of Yunying Özer

Yunying Özer, another disciple of this lord, offered him the following song describing his realization:

Single lord, wondrous and excellent,
Father, Vajradhara pretending to be human,
Your kindness is so great that your name is hard to utter.
Protector, no one is your superior.

From now until the heart of awakening,
Abide inseparably as the ornament of my crown.
Please listen for a moment to my song.

I met you, my lord, in my eleventh year.
Unconditional faith arose in my depths.
I had no wealth; I offered my body, speech, and mind
Without reservation and in song
Prayed that you care for me.

Lord father, you granted my request.
From that day until now
You have cared for me with kindness beyond recompense.
I've met a few holy beings,
But only you have introduced me to the ultimate nature.

I cultivate it through recollection and vigilance,
But my mind is often misled by distraction and bewilderment.

The fire of anger still blazes at times.
The water of desire is always turbulent.
I'm always wrapped up in a gloom of stupidity.
The gale of jealousy blows with fury.
I'm heedlessly crushed by the mountain of pride.

I'll never be free from this place of danger
Unless you tell me how to defeat my enemy.
Please tell me how to get past this.
Please kindly tell me how to quickly attain the fruition.

From now until I attain awakening,
May I always serve you, my lord.
May I see my mind's nature.
Bless me, father, so that I become indistinguishable from you.

The guru replied:

My son, so dear to my heart, and so kind:

Good and bad thoughts are innumerable.
They never depart from the expanse of thatness.
Other than self-arisen awareness,
Why do you pursue distinctions among thoughts?
Please be without action and meditation.

The thought "I've withstood this condition" is a thought.
It is caused by the fear of not withstanding conditions.
Please demolish the watchtower of hope and fear.

Other than resting freely in your own place,
There is no need to force meditation.
Throw away the terms "distracted" and "undistracted."
Any coarse or subtle fixation is meditation with an object.
In the objectless sky there can be no deviation or loss.

The king of remedies is devotion.
Impermanence and compassion bring the best progress.
I've nothing else useful to say.
Please keep all this in mind.

Then, Yunying Özer prayed for the accomplishment in this body of the celestial state in which one leaves behind no ripened aggregates:

Glorious supreme guide, leader of the dakinis' feasts:
Nowadays, at this tail of the age of degeneration,
Undisciplined people like me are unable
To reach the celestial realm in reliance
On the supreme substance sindhura
Without leaving ripened aggregates behind.
Please bestow your advice on me!

The guru's answer was:

My son, persistent Yudra Nyingpo:

Our Teacher, kind beyond recompense,
Gave eighty-four thousand instructions.
If his followers have the courage,
There is not even one of these teachings
That cannot be accomplished.

Supreme among them is the definitive secret,
The essential meaning of all instructions.
The three vehicles develop renunciation,
But the Buddha's dictates are really a single vehicle:
The fruition, great secret mantra.
It is, beyond doubt, infallible.

If you have the courage,
The instructions of supreme mother tantra are infallible.
The path is clear; it has been trod by all siddhas of the past.
On that path no sidetracks or errors are possible.
Don't hesitate through doubt!
Use this illusory body!

Don't fear samsara, this place of birth and death!

If you want to accomplish your own good
As instructed by the mother dakinis,
Don't get caught by the net of doubt.
Raise high the axe of resolution.
Cut the cords of indolence to shreds.

If you really are Yudra Nyingpo,
Accomplish the rainbow body of great transference
Through supreme leapover.[27]
Tighten the belt of courage.

If you want to change this body of aging and death,
Resolve to accomplish the celestial state.
Don't desire present comfort too much.
It's time you thought of your ultimate aim.
Don't be weak!
Don't procrastinate through laziness!
I swear that if you implement this, you'll accomplish it!
That's all this old man has to say.
Keep it all in mind, my son.

That same disciple then offered his realization as follows:

I bow to the feet of Lord Chökyi Senge!

Mahamudra, the mind's nature,
Has been pointed out by my father guru.
When I implement it in my being,
There is nothing to change or fix.

There is no difference in the nature, whether distracted or not.
Doubt, hope, and fear have been destroyed in my mind.
Although I have no need for effortful recollection and vigilance,

Effortless recollection seems to be present.

Because this nature is hard to realize,
Please provide further support.

The guru's reply:

E MA!
My son, so courageous in generation and completion:
When revealing your mind-itself,
Understanding alteration and no-alteration as indistinguishable
Is the realization of the astute who follow dharma.
It is hard to stabilize.

Indistinguishable alteration and no-alteration
Is definitive if realization is unchanging
And if distraction and no-distraction
Are also realized to be indistinguishable.

Although it is effortless, further effort is needed.
To realize your own mind as buddha,
Please abstain from the speculation of doubt.

In reply to Yudra Nyingpo,
I have written whatever occurred to me. Virtue!

That disciple then wrote:

KYE HO! Look, single father whose kindness
Is more immeasurable than even the buddhas'!

In this glorious forest of triple isolation,
This boy is immersed in the path of two stages.
One day, surprised by summer's drum,

I looked out and saw the dance of self-appearance.[28]

When examined, the apprehending self
Is beyond action and the intellect,
Inexpressible in words,
Free from the middle and extremes.

The variety of appearances is unceasing
Like dust motes in the sky's expanse,
But its nature is unchanging,
Always just what it is.

I offer this partial understanding to the golden ears
Of the king of thunder, so that the clouds of your great blessing
May be moved by compassion to resound with thunder
Both profound and secret, raining down the amrita that will
fulfill my hopes.
May you kindly bestow the melodious sound that shakes the
three worlds.

The reply:

Whatever happens in this or future lives or in between—
Good, bad, pleasure, or suffering—
Know your father root guru to be a source of refuge
To whom you may entrust yourself unconditionally.

The arising of genuine devotion
Is a sign that blessings have entered your heart,
And that the river of realization is overflowing.
The qualities of experience and realization have flourished.
The seedling of experience has sprouted.

The great poison of the kleshas is the best medicine and food.
Resounding with the beat of summer's drum,

It nourishes the aggregates and elements.
Because the qualities of experience
And realization have flourished, it is five-colored.
You are excellent, my son satiated by self-arisen wisdom.

The rainbow of external appearances shines within your body.
What need is there for our seductive foppery?
This egg of light—self-awareness—is enough.
Cultivate this unrestricted, undirected physical warmth.
Never forget this invisible, peerless, emerald feather on
your crown.
Polish it one-pointedly.

That disciple then wrote:

Dharma lord whose kindness is beyond recompense,
You've lovingly cared for me for a long time.

I've received all the deepest secrets of dharma.
I'm not fettered by doubt.
However, the dust of kleshas is piled too thick.
I've not achieved confidence in its groundlessness and
rootlessness.

Since I'm not misled by the doings of this life,
I hold the dharma of this lineage of accomplishment.
However, please give me instructions
That will certainly work at the end of my life.

The amrita of speech given in reply:

E MA!
Son of a good father, descendant of gods,
You've been linked to me by affection since your youth.

I've always taught you to be better than me
In your thoughts and deeds of the two traditions.[29]

I've introduced you to dharmata.
Other than encouraging you to cultivate it,
I think there is nothing else
For me to point out with new words.

Knowing all the thoughts of the five poisons that arise
To be the miraculous display of self-appearance,
Relax without doing anything.
What more can I say?

Until you reach the fortress of no-distraction,
Beware the danger of distraction.
Don't be fooled by the doings of this life.
Bind your being with pure morality.

Son, be unmistaken in your purpose; keep it in mind.
Always behave in accordance with good human custom.
Make your mind the essence of cultivation.
Conquer the enemy—your own continuum.
Support your closest relative—yourself.
If you can face death, you're successful.

I, your old father Chökyi Senge,
Think that I've completed most of my work.
To you disciples that I love with my heart I say:
Don't throw the Victor's doctrine, this wish-fulfilling jewel,
Into the swamp of samsara.
The care of this jewel has fallen to you.

This hope for spontaneous dual benefit
I hold thoughtfully in my heart.
Don't break your old father's heart.
Please keep this advice in mind.

The Song of Sherab Tsöndrü

Another of this lord's disciples, the disciplined vinayadharin Sherab Tsöndrü, offered his realization as follows:

NAMO GURUYE!
Infallible refuges, three jewels,
Glorious gurus, yidams, and dakinis:
I place your feet above my head
Beyond separation for all time.

This expanse beyond limit is the sky of great peace.
In it are gathered the clouds of impartial compassion
That send down the honeyed rain of wisdom and love
That moistens the soil of faith, diligence, and knowledge.

The harvest reaped from that soil is the discovery
That the mind is the ground and the fruition inseparable.
This harvest is free from the frost and hail
Of broken samaya and demonic influence.
Is this not due to the glorious guru's kindness?

Our peerless Teacher, Shakyamuni,
Taught the supreme path, the dharma of nine vehicles.
In essence, it is all a way to tame your mind.

From the beginning, samsara and nirvana have been of
one flavor.
The appearance of two comes from the mind mistaking itself
as a self.
The twelve links of interdependent existence arise.
The waterwheel of samsara turns.

We wander endlessly in the valley of suffering.
Although I and all beings equally

Want to be happy and not to suffer,
We are distracted and behave wrongly.

Causality is subtle. How could we escape it?
There are six states, three happy and three bad.
They are caused by imperfect virtue and evil.
Through the four common reversals of attitude,
My mind was led to the path of awakening.

To be protected from the dangers of samsara,
I entrusted myself, no matter what happens,
From now until the essence of awakening,
To the infallible refuges.

Omniscience is my ultimate goal.
I generated the two bodhichittas.
Recollecting the kindness of my mothers throughout space,
I followed the tradition of bodhisattvas by exchanging
My own happiness for others' suffering.

The natural realization and cultivation of emptiness
Endowed with the essence of compassion is the path of the victors.
These are united in the six perfections and the four means of attraction.
In all three vehicles, accumulation and purification are necessary.
The fine siddhas who've appeared ceaselessly
In India and Tibet like the Ganges' current
All touched the feet of holy gurus
And thereby achieved full buddhahood.

I first searched for an authentic guru.
You, my lord, like a peerless lion among men,
Are unequaled in qualities throughout Tibet.

I touched your feet, peerless protector.

You gave me the dharma of the supreme vehicle,
The means through which buddhahood is achieved in this life,
The unmistaken instructions of unified generation and
completion.
You also bestowed the empowerment which transfers wisdom
And the four profound symbolic empowerments.

Although, father guru, your kindness is beyond recompense,
My accumulated karma's a mix of good and bad.
As I've been unable to cultivate fourfold faith,[30]
How could I properly please you, lord?
This is my fault; who else's could it be?

Nevertheless, through my guru's compassion,
I roughly know right from wrong.
Although my diligence in cultivation is not great,
I've at least managed not to forget the goal of liberation.

To speak too much just causes fatigue.
The mind—what's called "Mahamudra"—
Is the ground, empty but unceasing in nature.
Cultivation of the path and achievement of the fruition are
mere expressions.

By looking at my mind, I saw emptiness.
What saw was the same as what was seen.
It was just vivid empty awareness.
It was experienced, but there was no knower to be found.

A lot has happened, such as being distracted and undistracted,
But when there was recognition through mere recollection,
I found the nature. All the effort of looking
And searching was included in recollection.

The nature of thought is to appear from the expanse.

In their nature, thoughts are neither good nor bad.
When klesha-thoughts accumulated karma,
I was no different from someone without instruction.

My body is slightly different from what it was.
I'm unable to speak of this further.
This is all I understand and know.
I've described whatever I remember.

Lord, master of wisdom and kindness,
Tell me with your discrimination whether
I'm headed in the right direction or not.
Please bestow your secret speech of wisdom.
If your disciple has overstated anything,
I request your patience.

The reply of the venerable lord guru Vajradhara:

The lord guru, omniscient of the three times,
Is Vajradhara, whose kindness is beyond recompense.
He is called "the root guru."

Our glorious, peerless Teacher, the supreme Shakyamuni,
Gave eighty-four thousand teachings in order to
Conquer the self-fixation of different disciples
And lead them all on a single path through
Skillfully presenting innumerable dharma gates.
Why should we not take him as our single refuge?

All beings are our parents.
We can never repay their kindness.
In order to protect them from the danger of bad migrations,
Generate the means of aspiration and implementation.
This is the path of all victors' children.

The vidyadharas and siddhas of India and Tibet
Have taught the supreme, unmistaken path.
You hold their rare and infallible lineage.
Its meaning is emptiness-lucidity with the nature of awareness.
Self-recognition brings contentment.

In the guruyoga of devotion,
Cultivate both contrived and uncontrived devotion.
If you cultivate them properly you'll benefit greatly.
Once all appearances and existence arise as the guru,
Your devotion will be unfluctuating.
The only guru is your own mind.
When it discovers itself, there will be no doubt.

Son, you've placed your hopes in your father,
And are content with the means I've taught you.
Your father's caring hopes are fulfilled.
As both father and son are content, we're both happy.

This is my urgent reply to the song of experience
Sent by my beloved son, Sherab Tsöndrü.
Because of my great age, what I've written is disorganized.
However, may its unmistaken meaning touch your heart.

The Song of Wanga

Another of this lord's disciples was the holder of the precious treasury of the three trainings, the accomplished Lama Wanga. He offered his realization in this song:

I bow to the feet of the glorious Chökyi Senge!
What we call "mind" or "Mahamudra"
Is really just self-aware, self-illuminating cognition.
I haven't found anything else to look for.

If these unceasing appearances of the six groups
Are known to be indivisible appearance-emptiness,
They are just the great display of the dharmakaya.
I wonder if they're not beyond rejection, adoption,
and remedies.

Such is my understanding up to now,
Through your kindness, my lord.
I request further supporting instructions.

The lord's reply:

Father Kagyu gurus, bless me!
Son, in the unborn expanse arises the unceasing.
It is liberated as the display of awareness.
This is the view, the self-liberation of what arises.
Please never forget devotion and diligence.
I offer this to my son Wanga in reply to his question.

The Song of Lama Karma

Another of this lord's disciples, the diligent practitioner Lama Karma, offered this song:

I bow to the feet of the kind father guru!
At first I mistook this life to be permanent.
I got lost in bewildering distractions.
Then I met you, noble lord.
I got all the profound dharma I wanted.
In the end, I am cultivating self-awareness.
I'm a little uncomfortable, however,
Because uncertainty and effort remain.
Please point out the definitive meaning.

The lord's reply:

The soil of my son Karma's bodhichitta
Has been warmed by his guru's blessing.
If you nourish the seedling of devotion,
The flower of the essence—mind, aware but empty—will bud.
It will bear the fruit of seeing its own natural face.
What need have you for doubt and uncertainty?
You are achieving something tremendous!
May all your wishes be spontaneously accomplished!

The Song of Kalzang

This lord's nephew Kalzang offered this:

I pray to the lord, my root guru!
When I try to get to know my mind, Mahamudra,
If I hold it firmly, I become heavy and tired.
If I relax, stupidity fills me.
If I leave it alone, I am carried off by distraction.
I ask for helpful instruction!
I ask for the kindness of correction and improvement!
I ask for blessing, siddhi, and transmission!

The instructions given in reply:

Son, Kalzang, your experience of practice
Is what it is because you're a beginner.
Tighten your mind and then relax it.
That is how to find the place of awareness.
It is also the ultimate view.
Therefore cultivate tension and relaxation alternately.

When your mind is wild imagine a dark green sphere below
  your navel.
When it's torpid imagine that a white HA
Emerges from your heart and dissolves into space.
Practice exercises that dispel torpor and wildness.

Directly cultivate whatever arises.
Don't wonder "Is this it or isn't it?"
A mind without hope and fear is the best meditation.

Cultivate the winds through the vajra repetition of the three syllables.
You will master wind-mind.
Son, may you unmistakenly realize your own mind.

The Song of Thrangu Yönten

The accomplished monastic, Thrangu Yönten, offered this:

NAMO GURU!
Precious noble lord guru,
Dechen Barway Dorje, hear me!

We bewildered sentient beings
Suffer ceaselessly through bad karma.
I ask you for a way to turn us all to virtue.

Karma and habits are so powerful that no matter
How clearly you show us our nature we never see it.
I ask for instructions on self-arisen pure appearances.

We will never escape samsara,
This bottomless pit of ignorance.
I ask to be led out of it by compassionate means.

Samsara is a city of birth and death.
There isn't an instant of happiness.
I ask for instructions on the path of the sugatas.

Sentient beings in the future
Will have no other refuge or hope.
I ask for instructions on seeing the guru's face.

Oh, Barway Dorje!

My body's aggregates, elements, and senses,
And all of samsara, have not appeared to be pure.
I ask for instructions on the pure appearances
Of the mandalas of wisdom deities.

Through bad habits I have not seen

The karmic energy of the channels, winds, and drops
As the sambhogakaya realms.
I ask for instructions on the three mandalas.

The habit of ordinary physical pleasure
Has not arisen as great bliss-emptiness.
Please demonstrate great bliss,
The sixteen downward and upward joys.

Samsara and nirvana are the great, all-pervasive dharmadhatu.
Not realizing this, we wander in bewilderment.
I ask for instructions on directly seeing
Samantabhadra, self-arisen wisdom.

The lord's reply:

NAMO! I bow to the kind lord gurus.

People don't see their own flaws.
They gossip about their friends.
Doing so is pointing a finger
Straight at their own flaws.

However, as I don't wish to turn you down,
I'll sing whatever song appears.

Don't look for others' faults.
You know how coarse you are.
There is no end to the faults one could list.
Don't look at others'; consider your own.

Others' faults need not affect you.
Your own faults anchor you to bad migrations.
Although you can't trust everyone,
In absolute truth dharma is infallible.

Direct your mind to holy dharma.
If you speak, speak the truth.
If you think, think of others' benefit.
Cultivate impartial pure perception.

Abandoning the ten wrongdoings
Is truly pure morality.
If you want to benefit yourself,
Don't do self-destructive things.

If you want to abandon malevolence and harming others,
Behave with modesty and nobility.
If you want to achieve dharmic perfection,
Flee as fast as you can from samsara.

The corpselike stupor of sleep is endless.
You are running out of time in this human life.
It is time to be courageous in meditation.

Desire casts us into the prison of samsara.
We make fetters of our spouses.
We are frustrated in our wish for liberation.
It is better to keep pure morality.

The poison of anger conquers sanity.
We disturb others unnecessarily.
Finally, everyone gets burnt.
Be diligent in the virtue of patience.

Pride is the basis of anti-dharma.
You doubt the dharma taught by your guru.
You vainly believe yourself to be more learned.
Unaware that everyone despises you,
You are fooled by your own cleverness.
You end up rejecting even yourself.
Every one of us must abandon pride.

Jealousy is bad karma indeed.
It accomplishes nothing and is self-defeating.
Once it's got you, everything is ruined.

It is hard to recognize our own poisons,
But we have to examine ourselves
And apply means to stem them.

Everything I've written here has been
Extrapolated from my own faults.

Now, the point is this fresh mind.
Don't alter it, change it, or sully it with the intellect.
Cultivate it by resting freely without addition or removal.
Don't prefer stillness to movement.
It is best not to hope for clarity
Or busily search for insight.

Cultivate such virtue in sessions and as much as you can.
Protect external and internal morality like your eyes.
Carefully avoid distraction of mind.
This is all the advice this old man can offer.
May it reach your heart, my disciple!

In response to the request of the diligent Yönten Ngödrup, this was written by Dechen Barway Dorje at the Glorious Hall of Mara-Taming Secret Mantra.

The Song of Töndar

The disciple Töndar from the town of Tridu offered this:

Vajradhara, personification of all refuges and the three jewels,
Precious guru of kindness beyond recompense,
Peerless lord, Düdül Lingpa, hear me!
Consider me with great affection.

Please rain down great blessings upon me,
Töndar, an old man in a degenerate time.
Cause the wisdom of experience and realization
To grow through my longing and devotion.

Best guide, root guru,
Dechen Barway Dorje,
Remain forever
In my heart's lotus garden.

Through undesigned compassion,
Lead me and all beings
To freedom from this endless
Ocean of samsara.

I ask for an introduction to
The nature of my coarse mind.

The lord replied:

Namo guru!
You, my disciple, have faith in your heart.
I will therefore answer you with affection and love.

With devotion, know your guru to be a buddha.
Have no doubt.
If devotion's yearning blazes,

The entrance of blessings is certain.

Your body's freedom and resources are rarer than jewels.
While you have them, cleanse yourself with prayer.
The fulfillment of your wishes, now and later, is certain.

Life is as impermanent as a candle in the wind.
Think of this and practice holy dharma.
Without procrastination, be vigorous.

If you don't mistake right and wrong actions,
The choice between permanent pleasure and pain
Is in your own hands.

Always be benevolent toward others.
Help them, give, and offer as much as you can.
Utterly abandon selfishness.
If you are without malevolence in thought and deed,
All your actions will become holy dharma.

Your protector, your root guru, is the lord buddha,
Vajradhara, pretending to be human.
Imagine him above your head.
Present devoted prostrations with threefold faith.
Offer as a mandala and without reservation
Your three gates, family, wealth, and all you possess.

Then imagine that the protector guru's blessings
Descend as a stream of amrita which enters your crown
And purifies all of the three and five poisons and the karmic obscuration.
Through this accumulation and purification will be achieved.

Light rays from the father guru's three places
Purify your three gates' obscurations and bestow blessings.
Pray with a mind of unbearable longing

And a body covered with goose bumps and tears.
Blessings will definitely descend.
This is the essence of all common and uncommon dharma.

The main thing is the awakened mind-itself.
When thoughts of external objects bewilder you,
Hold your awareness within self-cognition.
As that is freshness, don't alter it.

Just rest freely in it.
Don't delight in stillness and dislike movement.
Cultivate the nature of whatever arises.
This includes the essentials of all paths.

Don't reject and adopt through hope and fear.
Don't imprison that fresh awareness, that unaltered mind,
In the net of intellect and concepts.
Cultivate the yoga of skylike freedom, vast and impartial.

Correction and progress come from devotion.
The guru gives unfailing advice.
The disciple applies it with trust.
The result, omniscience, is placed in his hands.

Your acquisition of this body's freedom and resources is meaningful.
You've received a fine inheritance, the kindness of your father guru.
You, my disciple, have done very well.

I pray for the interdependence of us all, father and children,
Meeting frequently either here or later in Akanishtha.

These words were written on stainless, bright, white paper
By my son Mati Tishtha, in lamplight,
As they were spoken by Dechen Barway Dorje.
May dual benefit be spontaneous for all who see or hear them.

My Guru Taught

My guru, the personification of the three times' buddhas,
Taught experiential dharma that causes self-awareness
To arise in the yogin's mind.
I will speak of it a little to help your mind.

Now, at your parents' side, you are comfortable.
Not recognizing your own happiness,
You create your own misery.
Favored daughter, tame your coarse continuum.

Although you met dharma at birth your life has been wasted.
Reflect on all you've done up to now.
Your slight connection to dharma is due to your guru's
kindness.
Your entrance into dharma's gate is due to your parents' love.

The keeping of samaya and vows is up to you.
All dharmic and mundane achievements depend on
independence.
It brings present and future virtue.
I ask you to benefit yourself without pretence.

The young woman Namlang Drönma asked for advice.
The old man Barway Dorje gave it from his heart.

Cultivate the natural freedom of your mind's fresh
self-recognition
Without change, addition, adoption, rejection,
Hope, fear, fixation, speculation, or analysis.
You will definitely accomplish your ultimate aim.

Written by Barway Dorje at the request of Yutrul Rinpoche's daughter. Virtue!

Kind Guru

NAMO GURU!
Kind guru, I pray to you with devoted longing.
My clever, thinking disciples:
Entering the boat of freedom and resources,
Row to the island of instruction's jewels.

Disregard the waves of fatigue.
Take the best jewel, holy dharma.
This intention is excellent.

In order to avoid the storm of death
And the sea monsters of the kleshas,
And so as not to drown in samsara's ocean,
Raise the sail of vigor to the wind.

Cut the anchor of attachment.
Constantly blow the white conch of remedy.
Release the raven of the gods into the sky.
Wear the jewel of meditation on your crown.

Carry the gold powder of karma.
Reach the dry land of liberation.
Satisfy your dependents with fourfold generosity.[31]
All beings are equally your parents.
Be impartial in compassionate generosity.

Shave the head of your enemy, stupidity.
Bind the demon of greed with samaya.
Strip naked the seductress of desire.
Cut the poisonous snake of anger into pieces.

Chop down the water-tree of jealousy.
Flatten the sand hill of pride.

Imprison the thief of ignorance.
Hunt down the wolf of vanity.

Cast the dust of doubt to the wind.
Banish the blind men of hope and fear.
Elect wisdom as your leader.
Enslave the people—your thoughts.

Collect from them the gold and silver of experience as taxes.
Receive the tribute of labor free from good and bad
And wisdom free from adoption and rejection.
Build the temple of dharmic learning.

Commission the scriptures, the Great Perfection.
Perform the deeds of benefiting yourself and others.
Complete the approach and accomplishment of the
dharmakaya.
Bestow the great empowerment of the sambhogakaya.
Dance the nirmanakaya dance of beings' benefit.
Dispense the samaya substance of helping others.
Such is the great spectacle of spontaneous dual benefit.

The mantradharin Kunga Gyalu said,
"I need an auspicious song!"
With devotion, this wanderer Pal Traktung Barway Dorje
Composed this song of analogies for our ultimate goal
On a good day as it occurred to me.

Written by Barway Dorje at the request of my disciple, the mantradharin Kunga Gyalu.

The Song of Karma Chökyong

The yogin Karma Chökyong offered this song:

NAMO GURU VAJRADHARAYE!
Glorious heruka, lord of the hundred families,
Infallible refuge, supreme guide, Vajradhara,
Single father kind beyond recompense
Who abides in the lotus of my heart—I bow to you.

Your devoted disciple, Karchö, is a mere semblance of a
  Buddhist.
I will, however, describe my experience as I understand it.
This is how my mind-itself has appeared to me:

Sometimes the thoughts connected to my three gates' activities
Are caught by recollection. In that state
It is recollection that separates distraction and its absence,
As well as clarity and obscurity, success and failure,
High and low, and stability and instability.
The diversity of happiness and misery
Is like the changing of the seasons.

Sometimes I think of others' faults
And am defeated and worldly.
This makes me impatient.
Thoughts of the five poisons flow wildly.
When awareness returns, I think of even placement
And cutting through, but am powerless.
It is like riding a wild horse.

Usually, when cultivating my mind-itself,
There are no ideas such as hope, fear, success, failure,
Or intention. There is no "This is it."
There is also no unresolved doubt "This isn't it."

It is beyond both "This is it" and "This isn't it."
Nevertheless, it is indescribable.

This is a frank account of my own experience
As best I understand it.
Lord, single father, when I was in your presence,
Although I tried to tell you how my mind-itself appears,
I became unable to say anything.
Afterward, I examined myself repeatedly
And wrote this so-called "offering of realization."
I ask for a song about the Great Perfection, primordial purity.
Please point it out with profound instructions.

The lord's reply:

Glorious, peerless noble lord and protector,
Root guru—I bow to you from my heart.

Yogin, you inquired about experience and realization.
This old man will answer you.

From the fortress of delight in stillness and dislike of movement
The old herder without hope and fear set out.
He became exhausted in the valley of adoption and rejection.

Don't accept and discard too much.
Let the herder—self-awareness—stay put.
The mirage-waves of these appearances
Move farther away if you thirst after them.
They come back if you flee them in dislike.

The radiance of the five poisons in your mind
Is like the yellow radiance of gold—inseparable.
These kleshas, your mind's radiance, are poisonous
Yet they greatly beautify a peacock.

Don't see them as mental defects to be abandoned.
If you enjoy them as self-awareness's ornaments
Their radiance will arise as diverse wisdom.

There is no reason to stop your mind's coming and going.
The desire to know, the desire to flee, cause fatigue.
Look now! You see nothing. There is nothing there.
Don't look! If you rest in place, you'll see.

The restless hope for stillness
And the dull fear of movement
Make the deer of mind flee.
The mind is nothing; it can't come or go.

Your mind is awareness-emptiness; it contains nothing called "stillness."
Please sustain the nature of whatever arises.
If there is no goal there is no fixation.
Nothing to do is your mind's true nature.
If you're free from "This is it" and "This isn't it," you've resolved it.

Your mind and appearances have from the beginning
Been unborn; birthlessness is their nature itself.
Because they've no origin, they're primordially pure.
Their nature is great, primordial emptiness.
This is the ultimate meaning of the dharmakaya.

Its unlimited radiance arises as any appearance.
Its display arises as the natural sambhogakaya.
The play of its compassion is thought.
Whether coarse or subtle, they are all the play of nirmanakaya.
If you recognize yourself, the trikaya is complete.

In all your conduct, walking, and sitting,
Sustain your mind through mere attention.

Rest without artifice or alteration.

There is no "It is" or "It isn't" to be resolved.
There is no point in the exaggeration and denigration of existence and nonexistence.
If you never forget this pointlessness,
Your naked, ordinary mind-itself
Is Mahamudra, the Great Perfection, and the Middle Way rolled into one.

This is a clarification of your view and meditation, yogin!
The ground is precious morality, the ground of the teachings.
The path is generation, completion, repetition, and recitation: dharma's life.
May the ultimate fruition, the four bodies, be spontaneously accomplished.

At the behest of the yogin of profundity, Karma Chökyong,
These words were offered by Barway Dorje. Virtue!

A Reply to Two Nephews

This was written at Kyodrak in reply to the questions of my nephews, two brothers vigorous in accomplishment:

NAMO GURU!
Lord of all existence and tranquility,
Supreme protector of beings: I bow to you.

My nephews, saddened by samsara
And certain about dharma:

Having trained your continuums through the common path,
Vigorously accumulate and purify through the uncommon one.
Drive the stake of guruyoga into your hearts.
When you're happy, view it as your guru's kindness.
When you're suffering, benevolently purify
The bad karma of our mothers, sentient beings.

In order to purify your solidification of body,
Meditate on the generation stage, the unity of appearance and emptiness.
In order to purify your channels, winds, and speech,
Train your winds through the vajra repetition of the three-syllable mantra.
In order to purify thoughts within mind-itself,
And in order to cleanse kleshas, subject, and object,
Sustain your mind's stainless nature.

In the moment of that nature's self-recognition,
No matter what arises—distraction, torpor, pleasure, pain,
Clarity, stillness, movement, hope, fear, joy, or misery—
Rest in that for which it arises.

Cultivate such devotion for the three jewels and your guru

That you come to tears.

When you practice in such a way,
If driven by fatigue and torpor you start to fall asleep
Think about this:

Throughout a series of lives without beginning,
Ignorance and stupidity have put me to sleep.
This has created the cause of bad migrations and the seed of animal birth.
Now when I am vigorous in virtue,
I am, through carelessness, still imprisoned in samsara.
This body is my worst enemy in this life.
I vow not to let it control me.

We spend half our lives asleep,
Yet we never give up sleeping.

Hold your head up and your body erect.
Keep cool throughout the night and day.
Avoid rich and oily food.

Imagine your guru atop your head
Or between your eyebrows
As a water droplet as white as conch.
It is as cold as ice. Its vapor cools down
Your body, your mind, and all appearances.

Pray to your guru, the three roots, and the dakinis
Not to fall asleep.

Imagine that the place between your eyebrows is cold and wet.
Then imagine that your head gradually shrinks
Until it finally disappears into nothingness.
This will dispel brain ailments and lessen your need for sleep.

An alternative is to vow to grasp
The clear light while asleep.
In that state, recognize yourself.

In either case it is best to firmly resolve
Never to sleep in the ordinary way.

In order to gather the accumulations in all activities,
Perform the inner fire offering to your aggregates.
Clearly imagine yourself as Padmakara.
In your head are gurus and buddhas;
In your throat, male and female bodhisattvas;
In your heart, the new and old yidams;
In your belly, heroes and dakinis;
In your abdomen, dharmapalas;
And in your limbs, all beings as deities.

Bless your food, clothing, and such as wisdom amrita
With the three syllables.

Imagine the chandali in your belly as the offering fire,
The HAM syllable in your head as the melted butter,
Your two hands as the filling and pouring ladles,
The food and drink as pure amrita,
Your tongue as a tongue of flame inseparable
From the wisdom deities' mouths,
Your breathing as the mantra of vajra repetition,
And the thoughts in your mind as prayer.

For a ganachakra, bless the food and drink with the three syllables.
Imagine yourself as whatever deity you wish
With the deities described above in your body.
Consider eating and drinking a ganachakra.
Imagine the first portion as a delectable first feast offering
And present it to the deities of the three roots.

In this case, the intermediate and liberation offerings are unnecessary.
Dedicate your leftovers to the remainder recipients.

Consider the donning of clothing as the offering of raiment,
And the taking of a seat as the request to be seated,
Imagining the three seats' deities within you.
Apply these principles to all activities.
This is a profound way to make all your conduct virtuous.

Although it is hard to properly understand dedication and aspiration,
There is no contradiction in emulation,
As presented in the *Sutra of Three Aggregates.*
Therefore think "All this virtue accumulated by me
In the past, present, and future,
I dedicate to the benefit of my parents, all beings,
Just as do all buddhas of the three times,
The eight bodhisattvas, and the root and lineage gurus.
By my doing so, may all their aspirations be accomplished."

Aspirations can be made according to
Samantabhadra's *Aspiration to Excellent Conduct*,
With the thought "May my aspirations be accomplished like his."

At the request of Karma Namdröl and Karma Gyaltsen
These instructions on important aspects
Of yoga for sessions and between
Were written down by Barway Dorje. Virtue!

A Garland of Song Containing All the Profound Meaning: Instructions for My Noble Attendant

NAMO GURU!
You have accomplished with your three gates pleasing service to your guru,
The lord who shows the path to liberation.
You've undertaken the austerity to bear even death.

In a hermitage isolated from distractions
You are planting the victory banner of courageous accomplishment.
Through devotion, you've received authentic blessings.

Remembering the Kagyu gurus in your heart,
You've offered the service of songs of praise.
Young monk, you desire dharma.
You said to me, "Sing a song!"

My continuum contains neither generation nor completion.
I've no experience of drawing my winds into the avadhuti.
I've gained no confidence through experience or realization.
The channel-knots of my throat are not untied.
My speech does not burst forth as a treasury of vajra songs.

Unlike the Kagyus of the past with their great songs,
I've no ability to liberate all who hear me.
My words are merely amusing,
Like a parrot's MANI.
I'm unable to teach anything profound.

However, just so I not disappoint your desire for dharma,
This old man will sing a song.

I've never seen even a single decent sentient being
Among those of this age of fivefold degeneration.

They hear whatever dharma is taught, but none practice it.
The instructions are left in the books.
The books are kept merely for their value.
The profound dharma within them goes to waste.
This is so disheartening!

People say of the books they've seen,
"This one is profound; that one is great!"
Yet they use the tattered pages as a pillow or mattress.
There is no true empowerment, transmission, or teaching
  anywhere.

Like the tapering tail of a rat,
They become more and more deceived
By the mere memory of dharma practice.

Everyone nowadays, high and low,
Starts lying as soon as you meet them.
Everything they say just causes anger and desire.
They talk only of lawsuits and business.

The whole country's aflame with hope and fear.
Every cleric bears a householder's burden.
Spiritual teachers engage in crooked business.
Their mouths are stuffed with the lying oaths
They take by the names of deities.

They use trickery to obtain others' possessions.
They build their own high thrones.
They lie to their own root gurus at the sight of wealth.
They pledge their families as surety for a profitable loan.

Buddhist monks these days behave worse than dogs.
The shameless scoundrels then expect respect.
The mantrins drive themselves mad with sex and liquor.
All the yogins make village rituals their continuous practice.

The monks cavort with women in groups.
All the "realized" meditate only on wealth and profit.
They all destroy themselves through embezzlement.
They lie to their patrons from other communities.

They exact donations from their own communities through lawsuits.
They compete to become the worst example of wrongdoing.
They secretly break the main laws of the land.
They privately break the dharma laws of their vows.

They claim to be helping others, "benefiting beings."
They fool people with their pretence of goodness.
They falsify the dharma of sutra and mantra.
The three roots' blessings are disappearing.

Without the seed of omniscience being planted,
People claim supercognition of the three times.
This poisonous self-ruination is the true sign
Of the final five hundred years of the teachings.

It would be hard for even the Lord Buddha to fix this.
When I think of all this, I weep.

If you really want to practice dharma beneficial at death,
Externally engage in austerity with your excellent illusory body.
Internally meditate on devotion with fierce courage.
Drive the stake of profound instructions into your heart.

Serve the Victor's teachings through the vinaya.
Practice mantra for your own good.
Meditate on bodhichitta for the good of others.

Lower your head; don't desire pleasure.
Keep your seat; don't desire travel.

The ground of all dharma is the six perfections.

If you acquired all the wealth of a kingdom,
You couldn't bear to give away even a mouthful of food.
Have little craving for possessions, food, and wealth.
It would be best if you practiced fourfold generosity.

You've acquired a body with leisure and resources just
this once.
Having entered the gate of the Victor's precious teachings,
Don't fall off the path into the abysses of defeats and
remainders.
Please ascend the stairway of the three trainings.

Those who harm us were our parents in past lives.
Don't retaliate in thought or deed.
Secretly kill your inner enemy, anger.
It would be best if you donned the armor of patience.

Without procrastination, act as though on fire.
You can't accomplish dharma with an indolent fixation on
permanence.
Starting today, please quickly accomplish
Virtuous dharma through vigor.

Through the tranquility meditation of the causal characteristic
vehicle,
The deity meditation of the resultant mantra vehicle,
and so forth,
Cast far away a restless mind.
Cultivate unwavering samadhi as best you can.

Realize the selflessness of things and persons.
Establish these through the Middle Way and Mind Only views.
Gain good experience through the Mahamudra of sutra and
mantra.
Achieve the good result of the Great Perfection.
Generate the knowledge in which they are all rolled into one.

First hear dharma from your spiritual friend.
Then examine it by thinking.
Finally mix it with your continuum by meditating.

Resolve the ground through the view, using scripture and reasoning.
Experience the path through meditation.
Employ the means of unlimited conduct in the expanse of unity.
Enjoy the fruition, the absence of hope and fear.

The ground is the sugatagarbha within beings' continuums.
The path is the thirty-seven factors of awakening.
Accomplish the final fruition: the achievement of the unborn dharmakaya
For your own good and of the two rupakayas—unceasing and unabiding—
For the impartial good of others.

Now, in order to roll all this up into its main point:
If you ask "What is the view?"
The view is beyond the four limits.[32]
If you ask "What is meditation?"
Meditation is the unified clear light.
If you ask "What is conduct?"
Conduct is unlimited spontaneity.
If you ask "What is the fruition?"
The fruition is the absence of hope and fear.

Without subduing your naughty friend, your mind,
What we call "dharma" becomes mere worldly success.
That is unlikely to help in your next life.

If they don't tame their disciples' minds,
It's hard to call someone a "root guru."

If they're unwilling to undertake what is commanded,

It is hard to call someone "a worthy disciple."

If your thoughts and deeds, your three gates, are uncontrolled,
It is hard to call your external behavior "the vinaya."

If you're unable to bring your five poisons to the path,
It is hard to call your internal practice "secret mantra."

If your malevolence is unceasing,
It is hard to call your motivation "bodhichitta."

Unless the elaborations of thought dissolve into the avadhuti
And they see their own natural countenance,
It is hard to call someone "realized."

Unless the clear light appears as undifferentiated
  appearance-emptiness
Unceasingly throughout the day and the night,
It is hard to call someone "a yogin."

Unless someone has gained authentic experience in mind
  and body
Of generation and completion and has realized all samsara
  and nirvana
To be an illusion, it is hard to call them "a siddha."

Therefore, please be vigorous.

Internal self-awareness is emptiness, the *seal.*
It affixes the *seal* of wisdom on all external appearances.
All samsara and nirvana is an undifferentiated expanse of
  great bliss,
The variety of its display having a single flavor.[33]
This is the fruition of the ten levels and five paths.
Is this not Mahamudra?

Don't regard nirvana as good.

Don't regard samsara as bad.
The realization that everything within the three times is equal
Is the fruition without attainment or attaining.
That is the View of Undifferentiated Samsara and Nirvana.

The ground is primordially pure of external objects and internal subjects.
Without altering the six consciousnesses,
Cut through all appearances in fresh immediacy.
Through the wisdom radiance of the six lamps, the means,
Rest awareness freely on the path of leapover.
Bring the four appearances of the chains to exhaustion.
You will see drops, bodies, and realms.
The fruition, the four vidyadhara levels, is attained.
This is what is renowned as the Great Perfection.

Externally, trample on your fear in dangerous places.
Internally, offer your cherished aggregates as a feast.
In between, tame the gods and demons of self-fixation through compassion.
Bring your mind's five poisons into the expanse of emptiness.
Automatically complete the great accumulations by achieving the two aims.
Is this not the practice of Severance?

As all things are beyond limits, there is no assertion.
Faultless awareness remains impartial.
Is this not called the Great Middle Way?

All external things of the three realms are Mind Only.
Internal awareness in the moment is asserted to be real.
The Middle Way of the mahayana is beyond reality and unreality.

All things of samsara, nirvana, and the path
Are empty of their own nature.

Therefore all things, Empty of Themselves, are mere imputations.

Externally, all thoughts are unreal and empty.
Internally, all wisdom is absolute truth and real.
The fruition is without the slightest removal or addition.
Is this not the view of Empty of Other?

The ground is empty, clear, and not composite.
The path is unaltered awareness.
Taking the fruition as the path is beyond meditation and postmeditation.
This is called "sustaining whatever arises."

If you meditate on the rarity of leisure and resources,
Your mind will go to the dharma.
If death and impermanence pierce your heart,
You will be vigorous in meditation and accomplishment.

If you hear the details of actions' results,
You will know how to undertake virtue and avoid wrongdoing.
If you think about samsara's defects,
You will practice dharma to the end.

If you complete the accumulations and purify obscurations,
You will receive blessings and achieve siddhi.
If you mix your mind with your guru's through devotion,
Experience and realization will arise.

All fixated meditation is deviation.
Relax the fixating cognition.
All conceptualization is mistaken.
Rest in unaltered, fresh immediacy.

To progress, meditate on devotion for your guru.
To remove hindrances, eradicate doubt.

The root of all dharma is bodhichitta.
Meditate on impartial compassion.
When staying, be independent in dharma.
When going, be in accordance with others.

Without perfecting your own mind,
Never judge the minds of others.
Without measuring your own body,
Never regard the defects of others.

Dharma instructions received but not meditated on
Are quickly forgotten in the guru's absence.
You can't be a disciple of dharma
Without cutting through attachment.

When the child fails to receive the father's inheritance,
It is as though empowerments and transmissions were given
to a corpse.
Beware of that above all!

If you can't be fooled, you're wise.
If you're not bothered by your own death, you're the best
of Buddhists.

May the villages where mantrins like me practice be happy!
May monks like you remain in isolated hermitages!
May yogins like me accomplish our own good!
May teachers like you teach dharma for others' good!

This old man sings this little song in his home.
You Buddhists, go preach in the villages.
If these words please your ears, listen, all of you!
If their meaning strikes you, you may get angry!

Although I'm a bad disciple, my guru is good.
Although my experience is weak, the instructions are profound.

This garland of song containing the profound meaning of
all dharma
Was written in answer to a noble beggar.
Although I'm very distracted, I put effort into it.

These are not the dry words of mediocrity.
I've a little generation and completion in me.
I think there's blessing here.
Although it may not suit foolish ears,
It will suit wise hearts.
It may lack the beauty of ambitious composition,
But it will serve the father Kagyus.
It is the dharma inheritance of all my disciples.
Make it the essence of your practice.

My attendant, Karma Namdak, said he needed a song and offered me as much as he could with his three gates in encouragement. In response this was written by one crowned by long hair who merely retains the insignia of a yogin and vidyadhara, called Karma Jikme Chökyi Senge Mipam Trinlay Kunkyap, named Pal Traktung Gaway Yeshe Dechen Barway Dorje Tsal by deities and dakinis, at the mandala of accomplishment, the auspicious Shartse hermitage of the great college at Surmang, on a good day. May virtue and goodness increase! May this cause holy dharma to flourish everywhere! JAYANTU!

If Your Heart Seeks Dharma

NAMO GURUYE!
If your heart seeks dharma,
Give up samsaric activities.
Generate sadness and renunciation.
Cast the ten wrongdoings far away.
Undertake the ten good deeds.
Keep the pratimoksha vows.
This is the practice of the hinayana.

Meditate on altruistic bodhichitta.
Cultivate the six perfections as best you can.
This is the practice of the mahayana of characteristics.

There are three outer tantras which emphasize
Actions, conduct, and samadhi respectively.

The inner father tantra, mother tantra, and nondual tantra of the New Tantras—
And mahayoga, anuyoga, and atiyoga of the Old Tantras—
Are the generation stage, the channels and winds,
And Mahamudra or the Great Perfection.
In practice they are the same.

The essence of the view is the Great Middle Way.
Meditation is connate Mahamudra.
The Great Perfection takes the fruition as the path.

Their many and varied terms include:
Wisdom empty of subject and object;
Natural, ordinary cognition;
And spontaneously present nature, character, and compassion.

However, more important than their individual positions and ideas

Is their authentic meaning:
Resting freely in fresh, unaltered awareness.
The exhaustion of the intellect is the aim.
Freedom from contrivance and alteration is the point.

Exhaust self-fixation internally.
Develop devotion and impartial pure perception.
Be sick of samsara; generate compassion.
Without distraction, vigorously develop
Effortless recollection.

The emptiness of all things
Is beyond the elaboration of words and thoughts.
In emptiness is clarity's unlimited diversity.
Emergence and withdrawal are diversity and its single flavor.

When day and night are a single state, blissful and lucid,
The boundary between distraction and no-distraction is
exhausted.
There is no meditation and no distraction.
The achievement of the five paths and ten levels
Happens as described by siddhas of the past.

The speculative have questioned this.
How could the knowledge of those who've traveled a road
And the speculation of those who haven't be the same?
Therefore, devote your life to this unmistaken, supreme path.

At the request of my disciple Karma Yeshe, this was written by the itinerant yogin Barway Dorje. Virtue! May virtue and goodness flourish!

The Song of Karma Gyaltsen

The lord guru sambuddha's diligent disciple Karma Gyaltsen offered this spontaneous song about what arose in his mind:

Lord and protector of beings, buddha of the three times,
Wise and loving father, think of me!
You've blessed your son's three gates.
I've gained deep, devoted faith.

Lord, precious personification of wisdom,
I offer you what I've understood.
I understand that the trikaya is innate within my mind.
I offer you my experience of this as a mandala.

My mind as viewer and my mind as viewed are not two.
Abiding in that nonduality is one-pointedness.
I understand my mind's bliss, clarity, and no-thought
To be the experiences of one-pointedness.

My mind as viewer and my mind as viewed mixed together.
I precisely reached the natural ground.
This is just the beginning of insight.
On the ground of my mind free of duality
Experiences vanished like mist into space.
I think that is seeing the truth beyond elaboration.

My mind's diverse appearances are the nirmanakaya.
Abiding in that state is the sambhogakaya.
The absence of a viewed object is the dharmakaya.
In the ground, samsara and nirvana are one.
I think that is the revelation of the one taste.
I offer this understanding and experience.

If I've said too much I request your patience.

Think of me with great kindness.
Grant your blessing that your mind mix with mine
And that I realize the unborn.

In response to that offering, the noble omniscient guru bestowed these instructions on the essence of practice:

I pray to the lord, my root guru.

My son, you've applied dharma to your continuum.
You've asked me about your experience and realization.
Your father sits at the end of the rows of the Kagyu.
This old man will say these few words:

Once you understand the three times to be no-time,
You've realized the view beyond elaboration.
Your mind being without birth, end, or abiding
Is the meaning of the innate trikaya.

The experiences of bliss, clarity, and no-thought
Float in the ocean of tranquility.
The golden fish of awareness-emptiness swims there.
It is happy because it's free of the doubt "Is this it or not?"

The dual appearance of subject and object has vanished into space.
This authentic ordinary cognition
Is effortless and beyond the intellect.
Samsara and nirvana's hope and fear have vanished in their own place.

Indescribable experience has arisen in your continuum.
There is no danger here of deviation or failure.
The idea of samsara and nirvana has been resolved.

You are happy because the lie of hope and fear has
been exposed.

Externally, the seven precious qualities have arisen through
vigorous practice.
Internally, the dharma-eye's knowledge blazes like fire.
Whatever is empty is empty causality.
Whatever appears arises as illusory appearance and existence.

You understand the two truths to be indivisible.
You attain buddhahood through their inseparability.
You have no fear of samsara's abyss.
My son, you've resolved everything through self-awareness.
Please benefit beings impartially.
May you quickly become glorious, mighty Vajradhara!

This was written in answer to Karma Gyaltsen by Barwa.

Wishing for Liberation

KYE HO! Wishing for liberation, my children,
You've resolved upon renunciation.
Do not waste this rare and precious body of leisure and resources.
Employ it in virtue.

You've been accepted by your refuge, an authentic guru.
You've received profound dharma, the tantras' completion stage.
You've not just heard it; you've practiced it.
You've even seen a few signs of warmth.
Now bring experience into your continuum.

Guard the ground, morality, like your eyes.
Traverse the entire path using the channels, winds, and drops,
As taught in the oral lineage of the mother dakinis:
Pull them down, pull them up, pull them between,
And letting them fall into space, spread them throughout your body,
All the way to the pores of your skin.

Your mind is sudden, fresh, and unaltered.
Always rest in natural stillness
Without the intellect's interference.
Gently sustain the absence of fixation in postmeditation.

Always hold onto your independence.
Don't look at others' faces; look at your own.
Wrap your nose-leash around your head in freedom.
Be in harmony with others, without contradiction.

Resolve that this dharma is the ultimate.
Combine elaborate and simple practice.
Rely on mountain caves blessed by our predecessors,

Where your mind settles.
Vacation in the sangha's assemblies.
Once your mind is free, you'll always be happy.

Teach dharma to those who rely upon you.
Imagine your protector, your root guru, atop your head.
Be without duplicity in samaya.
Perfect nondual appearances.
Attain the great confidence of a mind free of hope and fear.
The benefit of yourself and others will be spontaneously achieved.

This was taught for my nephew Karma Gyaltsen Döndrup,
A disciple cherished in my heart,
By Dechen Barway Dorje.
May your good wishes be fulfilled in accord with dharma.
SARVA SIDDHARTHA!

A Little Song to Please the Dakinis

The great connate dakini Karma Ngedön Chötso said she required instruction. This little spontaneous song to please the dakinis was my reply:

NAMO GURUBHYA TRIRATNAYAYA!
Embodiment of the three jewels and all victors, Padmakara
  father and mother;
Panditas and siddhas of India and Tibet; and the lord with his
  subjects—
I bow from the heart to my kind root guru, who embodies
  you all.
May we all mature, achieving experience, realization,
And unobscured wisdom as taught by the victors.
May we not be deceived by kind words.

Queens of the gatherings of the expanse in the three pure
  places,
You've accomplished the state of the great mothers of the
  five families.
United in the flawless expanse with the glorious heruka,
You've perfected the seven aspects of mastery.
I bow with respect to the mother dakinis.

I'm an idiot with the form of a vidyadhara
Who bears the title Revealer of Profound Treasure.
My intellect is both irreligious and slight.
It's hard for me to correctly expound the essence of the victors'
  wisdom.
I'm unable to properly emulate the deeds of the holy.
However, as you're hard to refuse,
This old man will tell whatever his intellect has grasped.

If your actions are in harmony with dharma,
You will automatically accomplish noble mundane actions.
This leisure and these resources are hard to get and impermanent.
You will die. Consider the changing of the environment and its inhabitants.
Abbreviate your plans. Employ your three gates in virtue.
This is the ground of dharma. It is important.

Our "great deeds" do not survive even in our memories.
They are constantly destroyed by time.
Although we don't really understand
How good and bad deeds cause their results,
The rejection of selfishness and undertaking of altruism
Will make your thoughts and deeds pure.
If this is sincere, all your deeds of body and mind will be virtuous.

A pernicious desire for one's own victory,
Fame, and profit lies dormant within us.
It can ruin us; beware of it!

Always maintain the key observances of your three vows.
Unimpaired, they cause your qualities to flourish.
Focus on the essence of cultivation.

Acquaint yourself with unaltered, fresh wisdom of the moment.
Attentively perfect this until you are free of doubt.
Whenever doubts arise—such as "Is this it or not?" and hope and fear—
Relax on top of that very thought.
Abandon craving for, delight in, and adoption of good experiences.
Abandon disappointment with and rejection of bad ones.

Always behave in harmony with dharma,

But if you are excessively concerned with harmony with others
You will lose your independence.
You may come to resent your friends and relatives.
Love your enemies from afar, where they can't harm you.
Abandon excessive intimacy and resentment.

Always staying in one place is pointless.
Wasting time is pointless.
Rushing about in constant travel is tiresome.
It is hard to be firm and decisive.

In any case, dharma and mundane deeds are not contradictory.
It is necessary to integrate them.
The key is not to harbor selfishness within you.
If you are altruistic, you are independent.

Always examine your continuum.
Are your thoughts and deeds—your body, speech, and mind—
Good or bad, at fault or not?
What have you done? What are you doing?
What are your future intentions?
Know yourself and call your mind to witness.
Carefully distinguish between good and bad.

Always pray to your guru.
Whether happy or sad, entrust yourself to him with head
and heart.
Rejoice in others' virtue.
Don't become proud of your own virtue.
Seal your virtue and others' without conceptualization.

This old man does this to the best of my ability.
Holy one, glance at this garland of words
With your eyes of wisdom!
These practices are few, not many.
If you focus on these essential points, dakini,

You will achieve the good of yourself and others.

At the request of this wisdom dakini,
This was written by Dechen Barway Dorje.
May we all attain glorious, complete, natural bliss.
In the supreme realm of the glorious heruka's assembly,
Amidst a gathering of heroes and dakinis,
May there be the auspiciousness
Of a hundred graceful experiences of great bliss!
Virtue!

I Pray to the Guru Who Embodies the Three Jewels

I pray to the guru who embodies the three jewels.
Grant your blessing that my continuum accord with dharma.

In leading a life of dharma,
It is essential to abandon the conquest of apparent enemies,
Favoritism toward apparent friends, and boastfulness.
Live in harmony with others
Without losing the independence of dharma.

Lessen your concern with this world.
Don't desire a fine appearance or fine tastes.
Be satisfied with enough food to keep you alive
And enough clothing to protect you from the weather.

Maintain just enough wealth to support yourself without difficulty.
Behave as others do. Be your own servant.
In company, be tranquil and subdued.
Abandon from your heart acquisitive trickery and grudges.

Be inspired by renunciation and impermanence.
Never lose your stable commitment to practice
The dharma that will be of true help at death.
Bring your mind's thoughts of the five poisons to the path.

Don't let them draw you into ordinary behavior.
Grasp them with self-awareness.
Don't crave food and wealth too much.
Be content with whatever you get.

Always sustain this mind at natural rest in its own fresh clarity
Without distraction or judgement.
Don't choose one state of mind over another.

When a thought suddenly arises,
Relax within it and let go.

Hope for no attainment; there is no one to attain anything.
As there is nothing to attain, hope is useless.
Behave freely and spontaneously.
Your present practice is preparation for death.
You will need no other means at death.

Abandon the attempt to reach unreachable mundane success
At the cost of the dharma of definite success.
Meditate on devotion for your all-sufficient guru.
I've no advice beyond this.

If you listen to my words, they are advice from my heart.
If you keep their meaning in mind, benefit is certain.
At the wish of my disciple Könchok Gyaltsen
This was immediately written by Barway Dorje.
May buddhahood in one life be accomplished!

Radiant Space: Instructions for Retreat

May this be virtuous!

Primordial protector Samantabhadra,
Primordially pure guru: I pray to you.

All things are unborn from the beginning.
Cut through thoughts, clarity-emptiness.
Sustain their nature without alteration.

The six lamps are the display of compassion.
Without dividing them into subject and object,
Through the four appearances perfect the qualities
Of movement, attainment, facility, and stability.
You will attain the four vidyadhara levels.
May you complete the paths and stages
And reveal the fruition, Samantabhadra.

This was composed by Dechen Barway Dorje at the supreme place, Senge Dzong, at the request of Karma Könchok Gyaltsen. It was simultaneously committed to writing by Kagyu Tashi. May it be virtuous!

I Bow to My Root Guru Great Vajradhara

I bow to my root guru, great Vajradhara.

The realization of this mind, with its movement of thought,
Is just self-recognition, your fresh awareness itself.
Don't alter this through hope and fear of good and bad.
Don't wish for insight or clarity. Sustain natural freedom.

Always pray and recite the six syllables.
Be vigorous, remembering that you don't know when you'll die.
This was written in a moment by Barway Dorje
At the request of the devoted Gakyi.

Don't Waste This Body

Don't waste this body, so hard to get.
Remember impermanence and death.
Holy dharma is infallible. Trust the victors' speech.
Generate devotion for your guru, the essence of refuges.

Your mind is the essence of all things.
Sustain fresh self-awareness without alteration.
Since there is nothing to be discarded or added,
There can be no deviation or error.

Be disciplined with yourself and compassionate with others.
Never depart from virtuous actions with your three gates.
At the request of my disciple Könchok Rangdröl,
I have lovingly described how to apply the three gates
  to dharma.
A letter from Barway Dorje. E MA HO!
May this be virtuous!

The Divine Path Beyond Elaboration

On the divine path beyond elaboration
Bliss, clarity, and no-thought gathered
Like moisture in the sky of dharmata.
They resounded with unceasing thunder.

The lightning of no-distraction revealed
The hail of awareness-display cutting through
The seedlings of hope and fear.

In the garden of faith and devotion
A hundred-petal lotus of pure past aspirations
Smiled in effortless bloom.

The hero, self-arisen awareness,
Aimlessly wandering throughout this land,
Has made the good aspiration
To benefit all who encounter him.

Written by Padma, a son of the Treasure Revealer.

All-Seeing Manjushri Vajradhara

All-Seeing Manjushri Vajradhara,
Protector of all beings,
Great Splendor Tobden Düdül Lingpa,
Barway Dorje: I pray to you.
Liberate my continuum through the force of your blessing.
May my wishes be fulfilled in accord with dharma.

At the request of Kawo Tsodzay, this was written by Dechen Barway Dorje. Virtue!

Kalpika My Friend

Kalpika, my friend like my own heart,
You have been karmically connected to me since your youth.
I have given you earnest instruction and introduction.
I think there is no instruction remaining to be given.
However, I have three things to say in response to your kindness.
Don't forget them; keep them in your heart.

All composites are like magical illusions and dreams.
Especially, these aggregates that we cherish are fragile.
Life is impermanent, like a candle in the wind.
Don't deceive yourself with the assumption of longevity.
Right now excellent causes and conditions are present.
Don't waste these three gates.
Practice generation, mantra, and completion to the extent of your knowledge.
If, undeceived by the bewilderment of distraction,
You continue until death, that is enough.

This naked, unborn nature of mind,
Never without mindful awareness—
Sustain this experience like a river's current.
If at night you are unsullied by the bewilderment of dreams,
And in the day unobscured by thoughts of the three poisons,
That is maturity of experience.
Until these indications arise in your being,
Daughter, exert yourself!
Devotion without fluctuation
And samaya without pretension—
Don't forget these! Keep them in the center of your heart!

From our first meeting until now
You have never cast me from your mind.

That is the fulfillment of this old man's hopes.
I will never abandon my love for you.
Don't forget that! Aspire that we be inseparable!

Look at this single mind itself in the present,
Viewing it as indistinguishable from me.
Meeting and parting don't really exist; that is the nature
of things.
Resting freely is your mind's natural condition.
Give rise to certainty unsullied by doubt.
Practitioner of dharma, practice this!

This was written by the old yogin Barway Dorje to repay the kindness of my attendant of good family, Kalpikabhadra. May it be virtuous!

All-Pervasive Dharmakaya Guru

OM AH HUM.
All-pervasive dharmakaya guru, Samantabhadra;
Great bliss, sambhogakaya, principals of the five families;
Tamer of all, supreme nirmanakaya, Padmakara;
All three indivisible, lord guru, my refuge now and after:
I pray to Traktung Barway Dorje.

In this and all future lives, holy one,
Hold me without separation.
Pacify sickness, demons, adversity, and obstacles.
Increase life, merit, affluence, wisdom, and qualities.
Bring appearances, my mind, the environment,
And its inhabitants under wisdom's power.
Turn away the three and five poisons, enemies, obstructors, and elementals.
May all good things and qualities increase in this life.
Afterward, in the realm of great bliss, Lotus Light,
May I see the face of Uddiyana Amitabha.
May we all achieve manifest buddhahood as one group.

My instruction is to cultivate one-pointed devotion
For your root guru throughout all activities.
Recognize your own unaltered, fresh mind.
Once you've done so, don't appraise or speculate.
Relax utterly and evenly without hope or fear.
Sustain that clarity-emptiness as much as you can,
With a balance between effort and relaxation.
Always renew awareness with vigor.
Through this the qualities of experience and realization,
Such as tranquility and insight, will develop.
If doubt arises, rest freely within that thought of doubt.
It will be self-liberated.

Repeatedly describe your experience to your guru in order
to progress.

At the request of the maiden Dechen Paldrön,
Who comes from a family of dakinis,
This was composed by the old vidyadhara Barway Dorje.
It was committed to writing by my disciple Karma Chödzin.
May all who encounter this be held by the victors
And unmistakenly realize Mahamudra. MANGALAM!

The Song of a Young Bee: A Feast Song of Instruction

E MA!
In this wondrous, profound, greatly secret vajra feast-hall,
These diverse delights are well displayed for wisdom's enjoyment.
To this pure feast of heroic yogins and yoginis I invite my root guru,
Who presides at the feasts of dakinis in the three places.
Ocean of vidyadharas, please join this good gathering.

This nourishing food is of the finest flavor and symbolic form.
Its decoration is rich, sweet, and soothing to the throat.
This meat is powerful in its potency.

I offer drinks of thousandfold power
Made from the essences of sweet tree-sap,
Sugar, honey, fruits sweet and sour, flowers, and grain.
This supreme samaya substance, intoxicating amrita
Transformed into pure medicine through wisdom's power,
I offer to quench the thirst of vidyadharas, heroes, and dakinis.

I dance to express the joy of great bliss.

The appearance of thoughts is unbearably great joy.
Far from ordinary, they are the display of bliss and emptiness united.
When they arose, amidst their self-arisen self-liberation
I remembered the glorious heruka, the lord and master of feasts, my guru,
Whose great kindness is like that of Samantabhadra and Vajradhara.

Unbearably intense longing and devotion blazed.
I knew that whatever appears and exists is my guru's display.
I gained confidence in the inseparability of my mind and my guru.
I knew it to be self-apparent and self-arisen; it was revealed.

Ho! Within the external and internal expanses are the realms of all victors.
Their palaces are billions of clusters of spheres.
The chains of awareness are deities, self-aware wisdom.
The cultivation of expanse and awareness, inseparable and unchanging,
Is the great splendor of the most fortunate.

The bearing of body and appearances is the point of the generation stage.
They are not solid or substantial, but rainbowlike and illusory.
The bearing of speech and sound is like echoes and the sound of the wind.
It is mantra-speech, the noise of sound-emptiness.
The bearing of mind, awareness-emptiness, is the cultivation of the clear light.
It is wisdom beyond intellect or focus, and pervades all samsara and nirvana.

The view is impartial primordial liberation equal to space.
The meditation is self-illuminating self-awareness.
The king of conducts is without action, effort, acceptance, or rejection.
The view, meditation, and conduct are without fixation, like designs in space.

By sustaining actionless, unaltered, freshness in my life,
I've been freed from the bonds of elaboration, hope, and fear.
Happiness! Joy! My root guru's kindness!
Delight! Satisfaction! The auspicious, spontaneous accomplishment of the two aims!
I offer this to the ocean of the three roots and jewels!

At the request of my disciple Könchok Sönam, this was written by Jvala Vajra. May there be auspicious virtue!

The Sound of Great Vajra Bliss: A Feast Song

A HO! In the vessel, the avadhuti in which karmic winds are
purified into space,
Are the drops of wisdom, the great-bliss dance of a
water-moon.
This is the main samaya substance pleasing to the sugatas.
I offer this desirable, pure, supreme bliss.

From the expanse of Akanishtha, the residence of the three
times' victors,
I invite the self-arisen heruka, the glorious connate warrior,
The supreme principal of the dakini mandalas of the places
and realms:
Please join this ganachakra of great bliss and wisdom.

From the primordially pure charnel grounds I invite the heroes
and heroines,
Graceful with a hundred expressions of bliss-emptiness.
With conduct free from thoughts of clean and dirty,
Enjoy this ganachakra of sixfold satisfaction.

From the trikaya mandala of great bliss and the charnel ground
realms
I invite the dharmapalas, awareness-display performing the
three times' victors' activity.
Chop up the arrogance of those impaired by bewilderment.
Enjoy the food of heroes: the heart of self-fixation, hope,
and fear.

Into the center of the expanse of E, threefold liberation in
emptiness,
I invite enemies of the ten types, bewildered in the five
continuums.
Binding them with the seals of the four immeasurables,

I liberate them with the vajra kila of awareness-emptiness.

In the self-arisen place of nondual appearance and mind is
the yogin,
At ease in the great simultaneity of arising and liberation,
Enjoying the pleasure of bliss, clarity, and no-thought.
This ganachakra without separation between meditation and
afterward is beautiful.

Trikaya guru, from the limitless sky of the dharmakaya
Rain down the flowers of the four empowerments' blessings.
Fill the three levels with the euphony of sound-emptiness.
Bestow changeless, permanent, and holy auspiciousness.

In the mansion of five-colored light,
The display of great, primordially pure awareness,
May manifest dharmata appear
As the wisdom of expanse-awareness.

Increasing, may the bodies and realms reach fullness
And subside in dharmata's expanse.
Bestow the auspicious four appearances of spontaneous
presence,
Liberation in the youthful vase-body.

This was spontaneously written as the expression of self-arisen awareness by the lord guru's son, Padma Tsewang Dechen Chokdrup.

The Sunlight of Compassion: A Guruyoga of Blessing

Namo gurubhya! This is the continuing practice of the guruyoga of the glorious vidyadhara Lerap Düdjom Dorje:[34]

NAMO!
I and all other beings take refuge from now until awakening
In the guru, the single all-sufficient source of hope.
All beings without exception have been my parents.
I resolve to place them all in supreme awakening.

My body is like a rainbow, like space.
In the center of my heart's precious lotus
On means and knowledge—a sun, a moon, and male and
female Kamadevas—
Is the guru Heruka who personifies all things.
He is Chakrasamvara, radiantly blue like vaidurya.
He has one face and two hands which are crossed
At his heart holding a vajra and a bell.
The supreme mother Varahi is red and holds a knife and skull.
The father and mother dance with joy and bliss.
They are both in sambhogakaya attire.
His tigerskin skirt is loosened.
With the appearance of an enraged brahmin,
He dances gracefully with one straight leg and the other bent.
They are radiant in a blazing expanse of light and rays.

I respectfully salute you with strong, self-arisen faith.
I present offerings emanated by my thoughts.
I confess being unknowingly overpowered by the two
obscurations.
I rejoice in the pure virtue of everyone.

I encourage you to turn the dharmachakra of immaculate great bliss.
I pray that you remain permanently, stably, and without change.
I aspire that the fruits of my merit ripen for beings.

OM AH HUM!
In the dharmakaya's sky you are the compassionate sun that tames beings.
Supremely Great Splendor, vajra-heart holder, hear me!
Give me right now—not "soon"—
The power to melt the ice of my kleshas.

Your supreme activity is to play with the maras.
You are renowned as Karma Shribhadra Mangala.
Leader of vidyadharas, your bodhichitta and aspirations are powerful.
Gaze upon your disciples with compassion.

Your sambhogakaya is a crystal moon dispelling darkness.
Indivisible from the yidam, you personify the five bodies.
Gaze upon me, a cynic born in a degenerate age.
Personification of wisdom and love, remove my dark ignorance.

Your sixty qualities blaze like comets in the sky.
The array of your compassionate deeds is like the stars and planets.
Send down showers of blessing to ripen beings with bliss and warmth.
Send forth the shooting stars of your compassionate nirmanakayas.

When I sing this song of the queen of spring with longing,
Think of me, lord of the treasury of siddhis, like the lord of nagas.
Emit without thought rays of light from the jewel of your crown.
Increase beings' fruition of utter virtue.

Sky-bull who sends down a rain of blessing,

Resound with sixty holy branches of euphony.
Increase our experience of hearing, thinking, and meditating
  on the well-said.
Soften the hard, dry soil of our mindless, habitual bewilderment.
Kind guru, gaze with unobscured eyes on your devoted son
Who follows his father in all his births.
Bestow the great empowerment that transfers your
  compassionate blessing.
I pray never to be separated from you for even an instant.

OM AH HUM VAJRADHARA SARVA SIDDHI HUM

Recite that as an earnest prayer. At the end:

Single deity of deities, indivisible from my mind,
Noble lord guru, abide as my heart's essence.
Cause the darkness of my ignorance and kleshas to illuminate itself.
Open the hundred gates of wisdom. Vajradhara, hear me!

Glorious guru, a body like yours,
A retinue, a life span, a realm,
And a supremely excellent name just like yours:
May exactly these occur for us all.

Make that aspiration. At the request of Kyodrak Tulku Karma Kagyu Tashi, this was composed by Barway Dorje and simultaneously written down by Karma Dulwa Lhadar. May this cause all beings to be cared for by this holy guru.

An All-Inclusive Guruyoga for a Single Seat

NAMO GURU!

I take refuge in the sugatas, the trikaya gurus.
In order to place my mothers, all beings, in buddhahood
I generate the four immeasurables and supreme bodhichitta.

Above my head, on a lion throne, lotus, sun, and moon,
Is my root guru, unaltered Vajradhara,
In his actual form, resplendently clear.
He is the essence of all sources of hope and refuge.
I pray to him with unbearably strong devotion.

NAMO!
All the three jewels and roots and all victors without exception
Are contained in my root guru's body, speech, mind, qualities,
  and activity.
Your compassion is as vast as space.
The great clouds of your blessings send down a rain of siddhi.
Your deeds in taming beings warm all beings' hearts.
I pray to my root guru, the all-inclusive embodiment.
My mind has turned to dharma through your kindness.
Dechen Barway Dorje Düdül Lingpa:
I pray to you from my heart. Bless me!
When sick I dream of lasting health.
Old, I still imagine living on.
I think of death but strive for food and wealth.
I've bad karma and a heart of stone!
Tame my being with great compassion.
Hold me with the hook of able kindness.
Raise me like a child with your great love.
Tame and change my cynical mind.
Bless my three gates with your body, speech, and mind.
Mature and liberate my body, speech, and mind.

Bless me so that my every thought and deed accord with dharma.

OM AH HUM GURU SHRI HERUKA MAHASUKHA JNANA JVALA VAJRA SARVA SIDDHI HUM

Recite the prayer and the name mantra as many times as you can with strong devotion. At the end:

In order to bless me with great compassion
The guru emits white light from the OM in his forehead.
The blessing of his body is like moonlight.
It dissolves into my forehead.
My physical obscurations are purified.
I receive the vase blessing-empowerment.
The nirmanakaya is matured.
From the AH in the guru's throat red light-rays are emitted.
Like sunlight, they dissolve into my throat.
My verbal obscurations are purified.
I receive the blessing of speech.
The resultant sambhogakaya is matured.
From the HUM in his heart blue light-rays are emitted.
Like molten sky, they dissolve into my heart.
My mental obscurations are purified.
The blessing of mind is transferred to me.
The resultant dharmakaya is revealed.
From his navel light-rays of five colors are emitted.
The blessing of wisdom dissolves into my navel.
The equal, karmic, klesha, and cognitive obscurations are purified.
My body is transformed into the seal of a deity, adorned with marks and signs.
My speech and winds are the sound of the vowels and consonants.
My mind, with hundreds of samadhis, is the five wisdoms' play.
The svabhavikakaya is revealed.

Indivisible from the glorious guru, Mahavajradhara,
May I reveal unity.

With your mind, do not think of the past; it is indescribable.
The future is unborn; do not beckon thoughts.
Do not alter or remove present thoughts.
Let go of any desire for clarity or stillness beyond mere attention.
Whatever occurs is ordinary cognition itself.
Abandon speculation as to whether it is or is not.
Sustain undistractedness no matter what happens.
Pray to your guru and cultivate compassion for beings.
Be undistracted in this life, future ones, and in between.
If you sustain just that, great benefit will be spontaneously accomplished.
This old man has no instructions beyond that.
I, Dechen Barway Dorje, composed this to be easily understood
Out of my heartfelt love for my perfect servant Könchok.
It was simultaneously written down by the monk Lodrö Zangpo.
May it be advice befitting disciples' minds.
May they practice its meaning.

Clouds of Blessing-Amrita: A Brief Gurusadhana

NAMO!
I take refuge in the trikaya gurus from my heart.
I generate supreme bodhichitta in order to liberate beings.

In the sky in front on a lion throne, lotus, sun, and moon
Is the buddha of the three times, beings' protector, my guru.
His marks and signs are distinct and perfect.
He blazes with multicolored light.
He wears the attire of the nine vehicles.
He holds a vajra and bell, means and knowledge, with crossed hands.
His two legs are in the seated position of play.
He gazes into the expanse of dharmata.
He abides as Vajradhara, the personification
Of the three jewels and roots, and of all sugatas without exception.

KYE HO!
Guru, embodiment of wisdom, love, and ability,
I want to be freed from bad migrations and samsara.
I pray to you with unbearably strong devotion.
Bless me with your compassion.
Protector, grant your blessing that
My being is moistened by thoughts
Of impermanence, death, and renunciation;
That I complete all aspects of dharma practice without impediment;
That I perfect the qualities of all levels and paths;
And that I quickly attain the supreme state of the four bodies.

Recite the Vajra Guru mantra as a prayer. It is excellent to call the guru from afar. Finally, receive the four empowerments:

From the seeds of the four bodies in the guru's four places
Is emitted blessing-amrita, white, red, and blue.
It enters the top of my head and purifies my body, speech, and mind;
Their equality; my cognitive obscuration; and my habits.
I receive the vase, secret, knowledge, and word empowerments.
The blessings of body, speech, mind, and wisdom enter me.
The seeds of the supreme fruition, the four bodies, are planted.
Then my guru enters the center of my heart and arises as a heruka.
The father and mother unite in great bliss.
Through the flow of their bodhichitta I realize the four joys' wisdoms.
Then my guru becomes indivisible from my mind,
Appearance-emptiness, awareness-emptiness, clarity-emptiness united.
Mahamudra beyond the intellect is revealed.
May I accomplish the natural, true Vajradhara.

At the request of Lobzang Tenpa Rapgye this was written by Pal Traktung Gaway Yeshe Dechen Barway Dorje Tsal. Virtue!

A Note on the Visualization of the Uncommon Four Empowerments:

The bodhichitta which comes from the union of the father and mother guru heruka fills all seventy-two thousand of your channels, principally the avadhuti, rasana, and lalana; the wisdom of joy arises in your being. Then their bodhichitta fills all twenty-one thousand of your winds, drawing all karmic winds into the pure avadhuti; the wisdom of supreme joy arises. Then their bodhichitta mixes with the drops in all your channels; special joy arises in your being. Then their bodhichitta fills your entire body up to your pores; connate joy fills all the reaches of space. Finally, rest evenly in nondual bliss-emptiness. Imagine that the unreal, indescribable wisdom beyond joy is revealed.

Rain of Wisdom: A Guruyoga

GURU BUDDHA DHARMA SANGHAYA!

NAMO!
I take refuge in the three jewels
And generate the two supreme bodhichittas.
At the top of the supreme limb of my illusory body
Are a lion throne, lotus, sun, and moon.
On top of them is my guru, the personification of all sugatas,
all victors,
The heruka Dechen Barway Dorje Tsal.
His form is the sambhogakaya Padmakara.
He holds a vajra and bell and sits in the sattvasana of
great bliss.
In nature he is all root and lineage gurus and all yidams.
He is Vajradhara, who embodies them all.
Amidst an expanse of vibrant rainbow light and rays
of blessing
He is vividly clear, appearance-emptiness like a water-moon.

Buddha of the three times, precious guru,
I am stirred by unbearably strong devotion.
I pray to you, the one in whom I place all my trust.
Hold me with your compassion and bless my being.

The guru's body blazes with the splendor of blessing.
He melts in the fire of my devotion.
Becoming vajra amrita water, he fills my body.
My three gates' stains and my two obscurations are purified.
I receive the four empowerments.
May the four bodies be revealed!

View spontaneous awareness within whatever arises.

Rest freely, naturally, and freshly without alteration.
If the hopeful thought "This is it"
Or the interfering thought "This is not it" arise,
Rest within what thinks them.
Devotion alone is profound correction and improvement.
This was written by Barway Dorje at the behest
Of a worthy, devoted disciple, the yogin Karma Wangyal.
May it be meaningful!

Very Secret Avadhuti Guruyoga

My body is appearance-emptiness. Inside my avadhuti,
In the center of my heart, in the middle of an eight-petal lotus,
Atop a sun and a moon, is my root guru
As he actually appears, with the attire and locks of a mantrin.
He wears a lotus hat, a brown coat, and a robe resplendent with designs in gold.
His inner robe and skirt are white and bound
By a green belt in which is an approach-kila.
Of his two hands the right one overcomes obstacles
With an action-kila marked by a wheel.
His left hand teaches dharma, holding the stem of a lotus.
On the center of the blooming lotus are the book of the supreme vehicle
And the blazing great weapon of knowledge.
In his three places are the three syllables.
In the center of his heart on a sun disc is a white HUM syllable.
Its light dispels the darkness of all obscurations.
He is brilliant amidst the expanse of his own vibrant light of wisdom.

With the longing of devotion:

E HO!
Nirmanakaya, the nature of your marks and signs
Is appearance-emptiness that liberates by being seen.
I pray to you. Bless my illusory body.
Sambhogakaya, your euphonic speech of dharma
Is sound-emptiness that liberates by being heard.
I pray to you. Liberate my channels and winds into clarity-emptiness.
Dharmakaya, you are the only buddha,
Awareness-emptiness that liberates by being recollected.
I pray to you. Mix my mind with the clear light.

Svabhavikakaya, you are the wisdom that pervades all samsara
and nirvana.
You liberate by being touched, like an elixir that transforms
everything into gold.
Dechen Barway Dorje, you've appeared in my heart.
Traktung Düdül Lingpa, bless me.
My accomplishment of buddhahood in one life is up to you,
my guru.

And:

Kind guru, Vajradhara, know me!

Pray as much as you can, until you weep with devotion. At the end:

Then, the guru and my mind indivisible,
I relax in self-liberation without distraction or meditation.
Through this virtue may all beings throughout space
Simultaneously attain the guru's state.

At the request of many monks from the great Drupgar Monastery, such as the custodian Chöpel and Khenpo Chöpak, this was written by Barway Dorje.

The Spontaneous Vajra Song of Awareness-Emptiness: A Gurusadhana

The ultimate guruyoga of making devotion the core of one's heart:

NAMO!
I take refuge in the single buddha,
The inexpressible speech of nada,
And awareness-emptiness bodhisattvas.
I will dispel the miragelike bewilderment
And dreamlike kleshas of illusory beings.

My body, appearance-emptiness, is the rainbow body of a deity.
It is light, an empty form. In my dharmachakra's center,
Atop the lotus, sun, and moon of unfabricated threefold faith,
Is the holder of the unbreakable vajra that pervades all samsara and nirvana.
He is the actual body of all buddhas of the three times,
The Lord of Dharma, Padma's scion, Tobden Düdül Lingpa.
Compassionate, he is the color of a conch shell.
Loving, he has one smiling face.
Joyous, he has two hands. His right holds a wheel-kila.
His left holds the white lotus, sword, and book of knowledge, power, and benevolence.
Impartial, he is seated in the posture of regal play.
Unaltered and spontaneously perfect, he has long hair, a white skirt,
A coat, a cloak, a dharma robe, and an approach-kila in his belt.
His grand lotus crown which liberates through being seen
Displays the completeness of the nine vehicles.
Brilliant, he emits the light of a thousand suns.
He possesses the three vajras and the empowerments of all five families.

He personifies the all-pervasive and is beyond coming and going.
In his immaculate kindness, he is as vividly clear as the moon in water.

Through the interdependent means of the six outer and inner lamps
I meet you and salute you in united expanse-awareness.
I offer you the appearance of increasing experience.
I offer you the mandala of rainbow rays, drops, and light-bodies.
I confess infractions of the single, pervasive nature.
I bow to the great maturation of bodies and realms.
I pray that you remain in great undifferentiated self-appearance.
I ask you to turn the dharmachakra of spontaneous presence beyond the intellect.
I dedicate virtue in the expanse of dharmata's exhaustion.
Through this virtue may I traverse the four vidyadhara stages.
May all samsara and nirvana be liberated in the youthful vase-body.

KYE HO!
In this boundless realm of dharmata
You, my guru, are emanated by Samantabhadra.
Although to my water-bubble eyes you appear
As a rupakaya with material flesh and blood,
You are not my peer, an ordinary friend who does ordinary things.
It is certain that you are a rupakaya
Displayed by the victors in order to care for beings.
My faith and devotion are more than verbal.
I salute you and pray to you with respect.
Reach out with the long arm of your love,
My only father, my kind guru.
In appearance, in beings' eyes,

You are a friend who remains in their company.
You even seem to speak, teach, and listen as an equal.
Yet your behavior is not the emotional search for pleasure
Of ordinary grasping at objects and fixation on a subject.
You are definitely grabbing beings with the hook of bliss-emptiness
In order to hold them with holy compassion.
My longing for you is also not ordinary.
I pray to you with trust.
Don't let me escape from your able hook.
All beings of the six types are just like me.
Don't let them fall into the abyss of bad karma and bad migration.
With great compassion, be a mother to them.
When we think about you, you seem to love, feel, and need as we do.
You even seem to have thoughts of good and bad,
And to be attached to those close to you.
Yet, if we consider that you experience
What is solid for us as dreamlike and illusory,
It is certain that your behavior is how you lovingly care for us in your wisdom.
I pray to you with trust and devotion from the very center of my heart.
Mix your mind and mine as one.
I beg you to never abandon me for an instant
In this life, future lives, and the intervals between them.
May the devotion that sees whatever you do as good flourish in me.
May I serve you by taking whatever you say to be true.
When longing for the unity of the guru and my mind blazes unbearably,
Bestow supreme and common siddhi through entering your blessings into my heart.

That and:

Om ah hum guru shri heruka mahasukha jnana jvala vajra siddhi hum svaha

Recite this name mantra of supplication as many times as you can. At the end:

Most kind guru, abide inseparably in the midst of my heart.
I am a thoughtless, wild child entering the path.
Only father, guide to freedom, hold me with compassion.
Know your child's happiness and suffering, good and bad, in all my births.
Through the virtue of keeping as my vitality the samaya
Of the indivisibility of Mahavajradhara and my mind,
May I place all beings in the great bliss of awakening.
May I and all others attain the supreme state.

My noble attendant Ayu Bhaishajya requested this repeatedly over a long period of time. Eventually, in order to fulfill the hopes of those devoted to me, this charlatan offered this praise of himself out of obligation to them. It was written down at the feet of the Jowo Dorje Wangdrak in Upper Ga. May this be meaningful and auspicious. Jayantu!

The Fully Illuminated Essence: A Brief Guide to the Ultimate Guruyoga of Devotion

NAMO!
Guru, great embodiment
Of all the infallible refuges of the three times,
I pray to you. I delight in this essence and root of all practice,
The path of continuing yoga.

Lengthy expositions of the nature, definition, varieties, and levels of guruyoga are hard for nonintellectuals to understand and are unnecessary, since intellectuals will understand these things through study of the liturgy alone. I will therefore provide here only a concise guide to the meditation.

When you practice, straighten your physical posture. Keep your speech clear and pure and your mind cheerful and lucid. Free of torpor, vagueness, physical slouching, insincerity, and distractedness, maintain a clear recollection of the object of meditation. Of the three parts—the preliminaries, the actual thing, and the conclusion—the first is the preliminaries:

There are two of these, of which the first is taking refuge. NAMO means that you salute your guru and the three jewels with great respect of the three gates.[35] It also expresses devotion for your mind, which in absolute truth is the primordial buddha. Your primordially unborn momentary awareness is *the single buddha*, the innate trikaya. As the meaning of this is beyond verbal description, it is *the inexpressible speech of nada*, which is the unspoken, authentic dharma. Thoughts, in the presence of *awareness*, are self-liberated in *emptiness* like snow falling on a hot stone. We therefore affix the label *bodhisattva*, heroic mind, to *awareness-emptiness* within the state of not conceptualizing the sources of refuge, the person given refuge, or the giving of it.

The second preliminary is the generation of bodhichitta. *I* and all *beings* are like *illusory* people. Our *bewilderment* is like mistaking a *mirage* as water. Our *kleshas* are *like* desirable things in a *dream*: beyond what is to be *dispelled* and what *dispels* it.

The second part is the actual thing. It has six parts: generation of the support within the indivisibility of the generation stage's clear appearance and the completion stage's recollection of purity; the sealing; the invitation; the eight branches of gathering the accumulations; prayer; and recitation of my name.

The first: Your *body is the body of a deity*, *appearance-emptiness*, a *rainbow*like body of *light*. *In* the *center* of your heart, in your *dharmachakra*, the place from which all dharmas of thought are emitted and to which they return, is *unfabricated*, self-arisen *threefold faith: the lotus* of aspiration, the *moon* of awe, and the *sun* of belief. *Atop* that seat *is the holder of the unbreakable vajra* of indivisible appearance-emptiness, clarity-emptiness, and awareness-emptiness *that pervades all samsara*, *nirvana*, and the path. *He* does not abide within either existence or tranquility, and *is* in nature *the actual body of all buddhas of the three times*. Because he holds the source of all outer and inner pitakas without exception, he is *the Lord of Dharma*. Because he holds the secret, profound treasures of *Padma* who is omniscient of the three times, he is his *scion*. His various names include that with which he accepted the gradual pratimoksha and bodhichitta: Karma Trinlay Kunkhyab Mipam Jikme Chökyi Senge; the name given to him in the prophecies within his profound treasures: *Tobden Düdül Lingpa*; and the name given to him by deities and dakinis, as found in the colophons of his treasures, Pal Traktung Gaway Yeshe Dechen Barway Dorje. *Compassionate*, *he is the color of a conch shell*. *Loving* all beings as though each were his only child, *he has one smiling face*. *Joyous* with the thought of freeing all beings from causal wrongdoing and resultant suffering and endowing them with causal virtue and resultant happiness *he has two hands*. *His right hand* brandishes a *kila* marked by a *wheel*, the combined scepter of his yidams, Vajrakila and Yamantaka. *His left*, in the mudra of protection, *holds* at his heart the three families in the form of the *book of knowledge* marked by the *sword* of *power and the white lotus of benevolence.* As he makes no distinction between samsara and nirvana and is *impartial* toward, and free of acceptance and rejection of, friends and enemies, hope and fear, and happiness and suffering, *he is seated in the posture of regal play. He has long hair* and *a white skirt* because he is *unaltered and spontaneously perfect.* Because all his qualities are fully developed, he wears the dark red brocade *cloak* of overpowering all that appears and exists; the dark blue *coat* of subduing the haughty through forceful mantra; the saffron *dharma robe* of leading the six types of beings to peace and happiness; the green belt of activity that tames beings; *and an approach-kila* of meteoric iron *in his belt* as a sign that he has attained the power of force that liberates the vicious.

To expand upon the meaning of *his crown which displays the completeness of the nine vehicles*, this is the crown prophesied by Guru Rinpoche while in the form of a heruka in the celestial realm of Akanishtha. The root text of the treasure containing this prophecy of the precious crown of power, the *grand lotus crown that liberates through being seen*, is as follows:

E MA!
There will be a yogin of the supreme vehicle
Who possesses bodhichitta and engages in beings' benefit.
Without selfishness, pretence, or imposture,
He will possess the dharma of sixfold liberation.[36]

In order to accomplish authentic benefit for others,
Inspire faith and devotion in his disciples,
Change negative attitudes toward him,
And skillfully increase his activity of benefiting beings,
He will wear the lotus crown that liberates through being seen.

It will be round in shape and orange in color
As a sign of the pratimoksha's vinaya.
He will, like a pratyekabuddha, perfectly realize
interdependence.
He will be both as solitary as a rhino's horn and as social
as a parrot.[37]
He will be learned in the pratyekabuddhayana.

It will be decorated by jewels
As a sign of his benefit to others through the causal paramitas.

It will have a high and empty peak
As a sign of his achievement of his own benefit through
Holding the Middle Way's view and meditation in his heart.

It will have earflaps and hanging ribbons
As a sign that he will never abandon any being in his heart,
And that he will always hold all his mothers in his compassion.

The gathered clouds of compassion
Will rain down the purifying water of the kriya path.

The piping of five colors will represent the upayoga
Combination of the two means of view and conduct.

The petals in the four directions represent the four seals,
A sign of his possession of the view and meditation of
outer yoga.

The crown's five colors are a sign
Of the clarity of inner mahayoga.

The shape of a lotus with a vajra peak in its center
Is a sign of anuyoga's unity of means and knowledge.

The full moon as an ornament represents the mind class.

The supreme disc of the sun represents the brilliant expanse class.
The crown's blue center represents primordially pure
  Samantabhadra.

The silk ribbons of five colors are a sign of
The path of breakthrough and the four appearances of leapover
Perfected as the four vidyadhara fruitions,
The realization of the spontaneously present Great Perfection.

The vulture feather at the crown's peak is a sign
That the fruition of the king of vehicles has been revealed.

This crown represents the accomplished five bodies.
Anyone with samadhi and compassion who wears it
Will purify the obscurations of all who see him.
Their five poisons will be tamed, their bad karma purified.

In this body they will have long lives without illness.
Their splendor, merit, fame, and wealth will increase.
Seeing this crown dispels adversity and obstacles.
Through this crown's blessing the three roots will gather
  like clouds.
The mother dakinis and those with samaya will circulate like
  dust in a storm.

This crown closes the door to bad migrations and opens the
  way to liberation.
Even an animal that sees it will be liberated.
This crown of the victors which liberates through being seen
Will benefit all connected to you.

Always venerate and respect this crown
That possesses such qualities.
All who encounter it are fortunate.
Through good intentions, faith, and devotion,
Occupy your being with dharma.

This skillful means of the victors
Will be accomplished by their child, a bodhisattva.
It is an infallible dharma gate that will benefit beings.
These are the secret words of the mothers and dakinis.

Listen to these words and remember them.
Don't forget their meaning, fortunate ones!

As prophesied by the mother, the wisdom dakini,
In the celestial city of the expanse,
This crown is the vital support of a hundred thousand mother dakinis.
The glorious vidyadharas and bodhisattvas
Have placed all the mother dakinis in dharma by means of
This powerful lotus crown that liberates through being seen.
Do what they did!

This was actually said by Guru Rinpoche, in the attire of a heruka, on the twenty-fifth day of the Monkey month in a Monkey year.

Brilliant, he emits the light of a thousand suns and possesses the demeanor of great bliss.

The second part: He, clearly imagined in that way, *possesses the three vajras*: a white OM at the forehead, in nature the body vajra; a red AH at the throat, in nature the speech vajra; and a blue HUM at the heart, in nature the mind vajra. Because his five aggregates, five poisons, and five elements have been purified in their own places, the seeds of the five fathers and five mothers are clearly present at the five places on his head. From them flows a stream of amrita, bodhichitta, the five wisdoms. This purifies the stains of the aggregates and elements *and* bestows *the* complete *empowerments of all five* supreme *families*.

The third: In that way, your guru, Vajradhara, *personifies* all victors. He is *the all-pervasive* lord of all things of samsara, nirvana, and the path. His body and speech are the rupakaya, the samayasattva. His mind is the dharmakaya, the jnanasattva. They are inseparable and *beyond* the characteristics of *coming and going*. However, he *kindly* appears wherever he is imagined by those with devotion like *the moon in water*. As he is immaculately free from impairments, violations, and stains, imagine him to be *vividly* and brilliantly *clear*.

The fourth: Offer him the seven branches of accumulation and purification that contain all means of gathering the accumulations. Without leaving the guru of self-awareness as a merely imaginary object, encounter him directly and without separation as the vajra wisdom chains. The chitta lamp of flesh is the vessel of your heart, the abode of deities. The smooth, white lamp of channels is the path through which wisdom passes. As those channels end in the apertures of your eyes, those apertures are the gates in which wisdom appears, the distant lasso lamp of water. These are the three lamps inside your body.

The external appearances of wisdom, undifferentiated into subject and object, appear directly to your eyes and are not mere objects of mental speculation. The first of these is the pure lamp of the expanse. This includes the external expanse, empty space; the internal expanse, colorful light-rays; and the secret expanse, dark green like the circles on a peacock's tail. The empty lamp of drops includes those like fish eyes, like shields, and so forth.

Through the application of *interdependent means* employing those *outer and inner lamps*, the lamp of self-aware wisdom, which abides within your body and is in nature the deity and guru indivisible, will appear directly to your eyes as the vajra chains. *Meeting* this with self-arisen faith and devotion, *salute* it *in united expanse-awareness*. After experiencing manifest dharmata in that way, offer *the appearance of increasing experience* without differentiating between the presentation and the presenter. *Offer the mandala of* clusters of *rainbow rays*, *drops*, *light*-mansions, *and bodies. Confess* the *infraction of* not realizing that awareness alone is the *single*, *pervasive* drop or *nature* of samsara and nirvana, beyond division or partiality. *Bow to the great maturation of* all that appears and all that exists as *bodies and realms. Pray that* the guru *remain* throughout the three times beyond coming and going *in* the state of *great undifferentiated* samsara, nirvana, and path; undifferentiated now, the future, and the bardo; and undifferentiated *self-appearance*, all of it beyond acceptance and rejection. *Ask* that *the* great self-illuminating *dharmachakra beyond the intellect* be *spontaneously* and ceaselessly *turned*. In order to *exhaust* all the primordially nonexistent dharmas of conceptual bewilderment in the great, all-pervasive *expanse of dharmata*, *dedicate* unconceptualized *virtue* to the *traversal* of *the four vidyadhara stages* by all merely imputed individuals—you and all others. This is the aspiration that *all* beings traverse the stages of the fully matured, life-mastery, and mahamudra vidyadharas and quickly achieve the unity of the dharmakaya and rupakaya, *the youthful vase-body*, and transcend the limits of *samsara and nirvana*, utterly *liberated* from all bondage.

The fifth: Then, with the fierce longing of unreserved faith, call your guru—not just with your mouth, but from your heart—with the word KYE. Ask him to think of you by saying HO! With a pure outlook toward his body, pray that he care for your three gates, especially your body. With respectful physical salutation, think that this being of awareness-wisdom who appears to your eyes as your guru, although you presently treat him as a peer because he seems to live as you do, is not your peer in that he is altruistic, compassionate, and was born with the qualities of view and meditation. With the devotion of certainty, think that he is a rupakaya displayed by the victors in order to care for you. His love is like that of a father for his children; he stretches out his hand and protects you from birth, aging, sickness, and death in this life, and bad migrations in future lives. Pray that he do so.

With a pure outlook toward his speech, pray that he care for your three gates, especially your speech. With fierce longing, think that although he appears to befriend you and others and speak of good and bad as you do, he really has no solid, independent fixation on desirable qualities. He is caring for us compassionately and skillfully. Believing that, pray that he protect you without an instant's apathy like a mother caring for her beloved child.

With a pure outlook toward his mind, pray that he compassionately care for your three gates, especially your mind, in this life, future lives, and in between. Although he appears to share your way of life—loving, feeling affection, hoping, thinking of good and bad, socializing, conceptualizing, and craving things—he is without solid fixation. Because he sees all dharmas as dreams or magical illusions, it is certain that his behavior is the kind sharing of his disciples' lot for beings' benefit.

By praying one-pointedly to your guru from the depths of your heart with the belief that he is a buddha and that he is all-sufficient, there will no longer be any border between your guru's mind and your mind; you will no longer think of them as two things. Mixing his mind and yours, he and you will be beyond even an instant's separation. Because you pray to your root guru as the supreme embodiment of knowledge, kindness, and power, as an infallible protector and refuge, you will see whatever he does as good. You will hold whatever he says to be true. In the present, you will accomplish ninefold pleasing service to your guru. Ultimately, because self-arisen, unfabricated, unbearable devotion has been born within you, your guru's blessing will enter your heart. All the profound supreme and common siddhis will reach your hands. You will achieve the state of your guru, Mahavajradhara. That is your aspiration and prayer.

The sixth: Recite the name mantra as a prayer.

Third is the conclusion, which has five parts. It is appropriate to receive the four empowerments, if you wish, using the four lines of crying to the guru from afar. Then rest evenly within the indivisibility of your guru and your mind. Take the samaya of your guru's body, speech, and mind, cherishing them at all times like your life, without any transgression. Be without fluctuation in your devotion. Seal such virtues with holy nonconceptuality free from the reification of what is dedicated, those to whom it is dedicated, and the dedicator. Make the pure aspiration that you and all others achieve the level of unsurpassable awakening. As the words of the liturgy are clear, there is no need for me to explain them. However, the five divisions of the conclusion are crying to the guru from afar; resting evenly in the indivisibility of your guru and your mind; taking samaya; dedication; and aspiration.

Veneration of the precious guru is the source of all siddhi.
He is like a wish-fulfilling jewel.
May all who rely upon him attain the state of Vajradhara
And spontaneously accomplish dual benefit.

Abu Karma Zangchö, a monk from the north, repeatedly asked me to write something like this. Unable to refuse, I, the charlatan vidyadhara named Pal Traktung Gaway Yeshe Dechen Barway Dorje, reluctantly wrote this at the place of accomplishment, Akanishtha Meri Barwa, Karma Tenpa Tagyay Ling. May all who contact it reach the supreme state of the guru, Mahavajradhara.
SARVADAKALYANAM BHAVANTU!

A Rain of Siddhi: A Prayer to the Spiritual Friends of Many Traditions

HRIH!
Lord guru, root of all blessing;
Yidam, great treasury of siddhi;
Mothers and dakinis, whose activity is unstoppable:
I pray to the guru who personifies all three roots.

Three jewels, whose three secrets' qualities are perfect;
Lords of the three families, embodiments of power and ability;
Dharmapalas, who terminate the vicious:
I pray to the guru, the equality of the three bodies.

Second Buddha, lake-born Padmakara;
The eight vidyadharas and the twenty-five—the lord and subjects;
So, Zur, Nup, and the thousand and two great treasure-revealers:
I pray to you and to the innumerable other treasure revealers.

Our Teacher's seven successors, the two chariots,
The six ornaments, the bodhisattva Shantarakshita, Vimala,
Gayadhara, Smritijnana, Danashri,
Padampa of India, mahapandita Shakyashri,
And glorious Atisha: I pray to you.

Tilopa, who gathered the four rivers of dispensation;
The eight mahasiddhas; Naropa; Maitripa;
Marpa Lotsa; Milarepa of Gungtang;
And the peerless Gampopa: I pray to you.

Karmapa, omniscient of the three times;
Rangjungwa, lord of the doctrine in Jambudvipa;
The forebears of the siddhas of the four great and eight lesser lineages:
I pray to the Kagyu gurus.

Karma Chakme, the lord of siddhas;
Karma Dechen; Rapjam Döndam;
Dechen Lingpa; Barway Dorje;
And Ngedön Chöwang: I pray to you.

Glorious Sakyapa, the life-tree of the doctrine;
The three peerless ones; the seven consecutive Manjushris;
The golden garland of Mahavajradhara of Ngor;
And the all-seeing lord of Tsalpa: I pray to you.

Jampa Kunga, Tenpe Gyaltsen,
Ngawang Ledrup, Jamyang Khyentse Wangpo,
Jampal Tendzin, Ngawang Shedrup,
And Kunga Nyima: I pray to you.

Tsongkhapa, lord of Manjushri's teachings;
Your sons, such as Kedrupje and Gyaltsapje;
Chökyi Gyaltsen; our holy, victorious rulers;
And Zilnön Shepa Tsal: I pray to you.

The chakravartin known as Dung,
Uparaja, Indrabhuti,
Kaushika, Shuddhodana, Ashoka,
And the three forebears: I pray to you.

Anye Dampa, the great being Kunrin,
Rapjor Chöde, Kunga Yeshe,
Choktrul Gyaltsen, Choktrul Kunga,
And Kunga Namgyal: I pray to you.

All the hidden siddhas past and present;
And all the gurus, so kind to all, so kind to me:
Your qualities are inconceivable.
I pray to you with devotion and fierce longing.

All of you are emanations of the victors.
I pray to you all without partiality or sectarianism.

Anoint with the amrita-rain of your blessing
All the virtuous seeds in this vast field,
The good soil of our devotion.
Nurture the seedling of awakening.
Ripen its fruit, omniscient sugatahood.

At the request of those wishing for a prayer like this to the great, accomplished beings of various traditions, this was written by the person who was given by deities and dakinis the name Pal Traktung Gaway Yeshe Dechen Barway Dorje Tsal in the retreat hut of Anye Ngakden of Dzeda. May all who contact this be cared for by gurus!

Our Teacher, the Buddha

Our Teacher, the Buddha; the holy dharma he taught;
The four tantras—the essence of its eighty-four thousand sections;
The bodhisattvas, shravakas, and eight mahasiddhas who hold them;
And all the vidyadhara gurus of India and Tibet:
I pray to you with devotion and gratitude.
Bless me. Bestow supreme and common siddhi.

Written by Barway Dorje at Purgyal's behest.

Lake-Born Guru

Lake-born Guru, embodiment of the three roots;
Lords of the three families; forebear of siddhas, Lord Nupchen;
Your magical display, the heruka of great bliss,
Barway Dorje: I pray at your feet.

May I bind self-appearance by means of the six lamps.
May the appearances of the expanse, drops, and awareness
  become boundless.
May the four appearances of bodies and realms reach maturity.
May I reveal the fruition of the four vidyadharas.

Written by Barway Dorje through the interdependence of the diligent practitioner Samten Tso. May its meaning be achieved!

To My Teacher

Padmakara is an emanation of the three times' victors.
He emanated you from his heart.
You are a chakravartin among vidyadharas,
Drodül Urgyen Chokgyur Dechen Lingpa.

The single, delightful mother is the dakini Metok Drönma.
Her actual emanation is Dechen Chödrön.
The children emanated from your minds in the play of union
Are Wangchok Dorje Nyingpo and his siblings.

To my teacher, his retinue, and his emanations,
I pray with unbearably fierce longing.

May I and others transform our appearances into illusory
  deity-bodies.
May the bewilderment of day and night be placed in the expanse
  of the clear light.
May the unrelinquished five poisons become ornaments of the
  expanse of wisdom.
May I, the intelligent person on the path of means and
  liberation,
Mount the swift, vigorous horse of means and knowledge.

Spurred to a gallop on the blissful path of messengers,
May it bring me to the precious park of liberation.
Along with my guests, my parents and all connected to me,
May I be brought to omniscient buddhahood.

At the request of Ayi Rinchen Chödrön, this was written spontaneously by Traktung Barway Dorje.

Single Nature of All Victors

Single nature of all victors,
Glorious guru, compassion's sun:
I pray to you from my heart
With devotion and longing.
I pray that you bestow
All supreme and common siddhi.

Written by Barway Dorje. May it bring virtue!

The Song of Samantabhadra: A Great Perfection Prayer and Aspiration

The primordial protector of samsara and nirvana, unaltered
from the beginning,
Samantabhadra, the primordially pure dharmakaya;
And the spontaneously present sambhogakaya, the five
supreme families:
I pray to you. May I perfect the four appearances and achieve
the four vidyadhara states.

The twelve teachers of the thought lineage,
Vajrasattva, the protectors of the three families,
Garap Dorje, Manjushrimitra, and the gurus of the symbol
lineage:
I pray to you. May I perfect the four appearances and achieve the
four vidyadhara states.

Shrisingha, Jnanasutra, Vimalamitra, Padmasambhava,
Buddhaguhya, Vairochana, and Yudra Nyingpo:
I pray to you. May I perfect the four appearances and achieve
the four vidyadhara states.
The special close lineage from Samantabhadra, Padmakara,
Yeshe Tsogyal,
The father and son dharmarajas, Sangyay Yeshe, and Nyangben
Tingdzin Zangpo:
I pray to you. May I perfect the four appearances and achieve the
four vidyadhara states.

Nyenchen Palyang; Tame Gönsam; disciples; siddhas;
The lineages of ear, treasure, scroll-words,
And aspiration-empowerment:
I pray to you. May I perfect the four appearances and achieve
the four vidyadhara states.

The kings among jewels—the dictates and treasures arisen from the treasury
Of the mind, expanse, and instruction classes of the Great Perfection,
The wondrous apex of the vehicles—such as the *Vast Expanse*,
The *Heart Drops*, the *Life Drops*, and the *Mind Drops*:
I pray to you. May I perfect the four appearances and achieve the four vidyadhara states.

The *Quintessential Drop of Chiti*, the *Profound Drop*, the *Subtle Drop*,
The *Self-Liberated Single Letter of Samantabhadra*, and so on—
Atiyoga, the king of the nine vehicles:
I pray to you. May I perfect the four appearances and achieve the four vidyadhara states.

The lineages of ear, dictate, the dakinis' entrustment, aspiration-empowerment,
Profound pure appearances, karmic mind treasure, and predicted dispensation:
I pray to you. May I perfect the four appearances and achieve the four vidyadhara states.

Those who have attained the stages of devoted mind, opened family,
Great empowerment, great assurance, and perfect skill;
The embodiment of them all, Chokgyur Lingpa;
And Barway Dorje, the holder of his mind lineage:
I pray to you. May I perfect the four appearances and achieve the four vidyadhara states.

Guru Samantabhadra, Supreme Heruka, peaceful and wrathful deities,
Padmavajra, oceans of dakinis, and gatherings of each of the three roots:

I pray to you. May I perfect the four appearances and achieve
the four vidyadhara states.

Ekajati, Rahula, Black Maning, Shenma, Sokdrupma, and
Vajrasadhu—
The protectors, the display of the wisdom of
expanse-awareness:
I pray to you. May I perfect the four appearances and achieve
the four vidyadhara states.

The yakshi Shenmar, Barma Medong, the five sister-queens
among medicine goddesses,
And the male, female, and nondual displays of awareness:
Remove outer, inner, and secret obstacles.
Increase life, merit, prosperity, and the qualities of experience
and realization.

Through fierce sadness may my mind turn to dharma.
Through fierce faith and devotion may I receive the contents
of my guru's heart.
Through fierce fortitude may I cast aside mundane activity.
May the nature, character, and compassion be all-pervasive.

May I realize samsara and nirvana to be unaltered, great,
primordial purity.
Possessing the sharp sword of awareness and discernment,
May I totally cut through the chain of ignorance and
bewilderment.
May the absence of origination, cessation, and abiding in
the three times be revealed.

Through the three postures may my three gates become
workable.
Through the three gazes may I see the wisdom of the trikaya.
Through binding the external, internal, and alternate
with means

May I realize Samantabhadra, the single drop.

In the chitta lamp are the palace and deities, peaceful and wrathful.
The smooth, white lamp is the path traveled by wisdom.
The distant lasso water lamp is the gate through which wisdom shines.
May I be learned in the ground: their completeness in me.

Through solitary independence may my three gates be isolated.
In a mountaintop hermitage may samadhi flourish naturally.
Apertures for sunlight and moonlight, lights, and mental objects:
May I amass all the conditions conducive to practice of the essence.

The sky provides space for the outer expanse.
The inner expanse—rays and chambers of light—forms realms.
The secret expanse is the mind's emptiness, dark green light.
May the appearances of the pure lamp of the expanse be clear.

Drops and circles of light like peacock feathers,
As large as shields and as small as fish eyes,
The palaces of various deities, their own light:
May the empty drop lamp increase.

Like single hairs, knotted chains of gold, crystal garlands,
And pearls is the gleam of awareness.
Like the stability of birds, deer, bees, and a stake,
May the four appearances be perfected in stability and extent.

By binding the unmoving three gates with the technique of the gate
May the appearances of bodies and realms increase.
May I attain the states of a fully ripened, life-mastery, and mahamudra vidyadhara.

May I manifest the spontaneously present youthful vase-body.

At the request of my disciples, including Könchok Tengye, Daö, Tendzin Puntsok, Könchok Tsering, and Sherap Zangmo, this was written by Dechen Barway Dorje. May it cause all who encounter it to achieve the state of Samantabhadra, Changeless Light.

SARVAMANGALAM. Virtue!

Joyous Good Emptiness

NAMO!
Joyous, good emptiness
Bestows the best means of bliss.
Vajradhara, magical play,
Divine, heroic Manjushri: I pray to you.

Ananda who conquered the world's foe;
Manjushrimitra, leader of vidyadharas;
Kukuri, forebear of siddhas;
And Pal Traktung Nakpo: I pray to you.

Queen of great bliss, Tsogyalma;
Lord Nupchen, holder of the dispensation of Yamantaka;
Gya Lotsa, lord of power;
And Ra Tobden Dorje: I pray to you.

Shangtrompa, who attained the power of forceful mantra;
Rinchen Puntsok, supreme revealer of treasure;
Siddha and vidyadhara named Buddha;
And glorious Lerap Tsal: I pray to you.

When first accepted by the holy,
You bound your ordinary continuum
And took the name Karma.
I pray to Palden Chölek.

When you entered the rows where dharma is learnt
In the delightful enclosure of the sangha,
You were offered a precious throne.
I pray to Trinlay Kunkhyap.

The pure vessel of your external discipline
Is decorated with profound selflessness.
The victors' activity is fearless.

I pray to Chökyi Senge.

You possess the intelligent confidence of tradition, realization,
And the five common sciences.
Radiant and euphonic sun:
I pray to Nyenpe Langtso.

In receiving the coronation of the nine vehicles
Your being was anointed with the vidyadhara vows.
You hold the three jewels' teachings.
I pray to Mraway Senge.

When you practiced with fortitude
Profound and secret generation and completion,
Deities and dakinis named you.
I pray to Pal Traktung Dorje.

Your nature, lord, is Samantabhadra.
Supreme guru, you are the glorious heruka.
In secrecy, you abide in the celestial state.
I pray to Gaway Yeshe.

Commanded by the glorious Lake-Born Guru,
Prophesied in changeless symbols,
Great bliss hero of lotus family:
I pray to Barway Dorje.

Your body is the sangha, your speech holy dharma.
Your mind is indistinguishable from a buddha's.
I pray to you as the essence of all the three jewels.
Look upon me with compassion.

You are the root of blessing, siddhi, and activity.
You are the glorious embodiment of all gurus,
Yidams, dakinis, and dharmapalas.
I pray to you. Bless me.

Dharmakaya, sambhogakaya, nirmanakaya,
Svabhavikakaya, and jnanakaya:
You personify the five bodies, the four, and the three.
I pray to you. Bestow the four empowerments' siddhis.

May I be able to plough the ground, the soil of my being.
On the path may I grow the seedling of wisdom.
May the fruition, the harvest of freedom, be perfect.
May I serve it as a feast for my mothers, those to be tamed.

Although I am a mass of faults and without a sesame seed's worth of virtue, holy beings—themselves devoid of faults—see pebbles as gold. Unable to refuse the request of the wise, realized, and learned guru Jampal Zangpo, this song was written spontaneously in lamplight, and while I was drunk, by the one named by deities and dakinis Pal Traktung Gaway Yeshe Dechen Barway Dorje. Even though they were my past births, praying to holy beings will lead to qualities. The description of my present state is mere poetic exaggeration. May this bring virtue!

Manjushri, Wise Wheel of Stability

Manjushri, wise wheel of stability,
In the presence of the teacher, you were the bodhisattva Marutse;
Splendor of all gatherings of forceful mantra, you are Yamantaka.
I pray to the great embodiment of body.

From the inexhaustible wheel of ornamentation of Padmakara's three secrets,
You are both the great minister Dorje Tritsun and Tsogyal, celestial Sarasvati.
I pray to their indivisible, compassionate basis of emanation.

Manjushrimitra, the rainbow body of India;
Naropa, the supremely learned lord of siddhas;
Shakyapa, the translator from Tibet;
I pray to the garland of the learned and attained.

Dumgya Shangtrom and Shepa Dorje;
Glorious Sönam Yeshe, who perfected abandonment and realization;
Sönam Gyurme; glorious Sönam Drup:
I pray to the holders of the supreme doctrine.

Sönam Gyurme; glorious Sungrap Gyamtso;
Mingyur Dorje, the emanation of Palgyi Senge;
Guru Traktung Nakpo, who appeared in the past; and so forth—
I pray to the emanations of them all embodied as one.

Karma Sungrap Trinlay Rapgyay
And Tobden Düdül Lingpa, the lord of profound treasure,
Traktung Dechen Barway Dorje —

I pray to you one-pointedly with the utmost respect.

The water-moon dance, the play of one and many —
The display of victors and their children is inconceivable.
Since it is beyond the limits of reckoning,
Your life is inconceivable — I pray to you.

Bless your child who, recollecting the guru's life as it is,
Prays with unfluctuating threefold faith and devotion.
May I be inseparable from you, holy one.

At the request of the supreme guides Gartrul Rinpoche and Abo Rinpoche, this was written by Dechen Barway Dorje at Palung Pungri and offered as an example of how foolish it is to praise oneself. May it bring virtue!

A Beautiful Garland of Flowers: A Prayer to Successive Births

OM AH HUM!
Samantabhadra, the forebear of all trikaya victors;
Vajradhara, the embodiment of the five bodies;
Bhagavat Manjushri, the father of all victors;
Lake-Born Padmakara, the embodiment of the trikaya;
Vajradharma, the leader of all vidyadharas;
Vajrasattva, the holder of the treasury of primordially perfect mind;
And Garap Dorje, the forebear of all siddhas:
I pray to the supreme teachers.
Grant your blessing that my continuum accord with dharma.

Manjushrimitra, the vidyadhara of body;
Marutse, the first among bodhisattvas;
King Katun Nakpo, the siddha of forceful mantra;
And Lord Nupchen, the sun of the ancient translations:
I pray to the succession of blessed mind.
Grant your blessing that my continuum accord with dharma.

Tsuklak Palge, the holder of the store of profound treasure;
Great, powerful Shangtrom Dorje Bar;
Mila Shepa Dorje, the siddha;
Tsogyal, the leader of celestial dakinis;
Dakini Kunga Bum, the holder of the store of treasure;
And Drimay Kunga, the master of profound treasure:
I pray to the succession of various births.
Grant your blessing that my continuum accord with dharma.

Punyajnana, the master of samadhi;
Lord sugata Sönam Gyurmay Nyingpo;
Karma Rikdzin; Sungrap Gyamtso;

Mingyur Rölpa; and glorious Trinlay Rapgyay:
I pray to the garland of successive births.
Grant your blessing that my continuum accord with dharma.

Your past aspiration for degenerate beings
Has made you a timely lord of profound treasure.
Great Splendor Tobden Düdül Lingpa Tsal,
Dechen Barway Dorje, I pray to you.

Grant your blessing that my continuum accord with dharma,
That my pure intentions and deeds succeed without effort,
And that I gain the ability to place all beings without
  exception
In the state of Vajradhara.

In all my births may non-dharmic thoughts never arise.
May even the names of adversity and affliction be not heard.
May I never be seduced by the mara of distraction.

In the city of the wisdom dakinis' feasts,
The gathering of the good celestial ones,
May I become a heruka in the full youthful bloom of
  great bliss,
Immaculately united with the queen and outshining
All things of both samsara and nirvana.

Gracefully dancing with illusory empty forms,
May I enjoy all appearances and phenomena
As sense pleasures of great bliss without attachment.
May I quickly become the lord of the four bodies,
  Mahavajradhara.

The wisdom dakini Urgyen Kalzang Chökyi Drölma gazed upon me, an insignificant fool, with eyes that see trash as gold and repeatedly asked me to write a prayer. Unable to refuse, this old mantrin—even though the existence of the slightest virtue within me is improbable—wrote this in order to appeal to the victors and their children, the gurus, for rescue. It was composed in an encampment at the foot of the great god Yikgyal's mountain and immediately written down by Karma Dulwa. May it bring virtue!

You Attained the Supreme Siddhi of the Lord of Speech

NAMO GURU!
You attained the supreme siddhi of the Lord of Speech
And became Manjushrimitra, the vidyadhara of mahamudra.
Lord Nupchen, you abide in the level of Utter Luminosity.
I pray at the feet of Sangyay Yeshe.

Noble Vajra Throne atop a sun and moon,
Glorious heruka Jnanasiddhi,
Shepa Dorje, Dumgya Shangtrom,
And the splendid garland of your births: I pray to you.

You are now beings' protector, Padma's heart son who opens
The doors to places and treasure, outshining appearances.
Traktung Gaway Yeshe, Düdül Lingpa, Dechen Barway Dorje:
I pray to you.

Pacify adversity and obstacles of my three gates.
Grant me now your blessing and siddhi so that
My thoughts and deeds may be pure and accord with dharma.
May you care for me, guru, without separation.

At the behest of Karma Mangala, this was written by Barway Dorje.

All-Seeing Manjushri

OM AH HUM!
All-seeing Manjushri; Yamantaka;
Manjushrimitra; Sangyay Yeshe;
Dumgya Shangtrom; Gyatön; Shepa Dorje;
And your splendid garland of births: I pray to you.

Blessed by dakinis, you mastered appearances and mind.
Through Padma's siddhi, you tame beings with treasure.
Your activity is the timely awakening of your aspirations.
I pray to Dechen Barway Dorje.

Through your compassion may I be able to sustain
Without any doubt the unaltered, fresh recognition
Of this unborn mind of mine, resting freely,
Unsullied by fabrication or intellectualization.
Having traveled the path of natural, free self-recognition,
May I discover fruition Mahamudra.

At the request of Lozang Menla, this was written by Barway Dorje.

Dharmakaya Amitabha

OM AH HUM!
Dharmakaya Amitabha; sambhogakaya Avalokita;
Nirmanakaya Padmakara; vidyadharas of India and Tibet;
The hundred great treasure-revealers; and the thousand and
two lesser ones:
I pray to the gurus of the lineage of blessing.
All-seeing Manjushri; bodhisattva Marutse;
Manjushrimitra; the supreme scholar Naropa;
Sangyay Yeshe; and Shepa Dorje:
I pray to your births as a siddha.

Vajradhara, Barway Dorje,
You tame beings hard to tame.
Don't stop! Bless me now!
Cause my being to be freed by dharma.

Rest freely in the mere natural recognition of your mind,
Merely sustaining whatever arises.
Do not get lost in selfish speculation.
Do not delight in stillness or fear movement.
Do not doubt, wonder, or hope for clarity.
Be content with attention to whatever happens.
At the behest of my disciple Samo,
Barway Dorje wrote this in the state of whatever arose.

The Guru's Body

The guru's body contains all the trikaya sugatas.
Your supreme speech is the three vehicles of dharma that tame
everyone.
Your mind is a profound, secret treasury of powerful
compassion.
I pray that you kindly consider this supplication.

You are no other than the heruka Great Splendor,
A kind, glorious protector of beings.
Palbar Tobden Nakpo Düdül Lingpa,
Glorious lord, supreme guru: I pray to you.

Free from any stain of dualistic thinking,
You have attained nondual wisdom,
And subdue the habit of dual appearance by means of
emptiness.
Grant your blessing that the bewilderment of duality
be purified.

Written by Barway Dorje at the request of those with faith. Virtue!

Kind, Kind Root Guru

NAMO!
Kind, kind root guru,
We have long been connected through deep aspiration.
You are committed to kindness; don't abandon me now!
Kind, single father: regard me with wisdom.

I am tormented by chains of karma and kleshas.
I am ignorant, stupid, and infantile.
I may be swept away by the waves of my suffering in the ocean of samsara.
Compassionate one, grasp me with the hook of your kindness.

When I embark on the path of the essence, supreme means,
My heart may be poisoned by the demon of pointless depression.
I may sink into the quicksand of distraction and laziness.
Kind one, extend the long arm of your power.

In the darkness of my obscurations' clouds,
I do not see the authentic essence, absolute truth.
I wander about, blinded by self-fixation.
One with blessing, grant me eyes of wisdom.

Your devoted child prays to you from afar.
Please hold me with great compassion.
Now, later, between, and always,
Hold me, beings' protector, supreme guru.
Beyond a moment's separation,
Grant the blessing of your mind uniting with mine.

Written by Barway Dorje at the request of a young woman named Tseyang. Virtue!

The Guru's Mind

OM AH HUM!
The guru's mind contains all buddhas.
The guru's speech contains all dharma.
The guru's body contains all the sangha.
The guru's qualities contain all yidams.
The guru's activity contains all dakinis and dharmapalas.
The guru, the heruka, is utterly complete.

Traktung Gaway Yeshe
Dechen Barway Dorje:
I pray to you; bless me!

Through the indivisibility of
My awareness and my guru
May I realize absolute truth,
Mahamudra.

The practice is to recognize fresh awareness within whatever arises.
Sustain it naturally without alteration or meditation.
Affix no patches of opinion or desire for experience.
Sustain your nature without hope or fear.
At all times cultivate devotion, vigor, and revulsion.
At the behest of the custodians
Karma Özer and Sönam Puntsok,
This was quickly written by Barway Dorje.

Changeless Dharmakaya

Changeless dharmakaya, sugata Vajradhara;
Ceaseless holder of the teachings, Mraway Senge;
Unbewildered great bliss, Gaway Yeshe:
I pray at the feet of Barway Dorje.

Manjushrimitra; Gungtangpa, friend of beings;
Sangyay Yeshe; famous Dumgya Shangtrom:
Nowadays you are the heruka Gaway Yeshe.
I pray to Dechen Barway Dorje.

Glorious guru, may I possess a body like yours,
A retinue, a life span, a realm,
And a supreme name like yours.
May I become just like you.

I wrote this at the request of the faithful Nyendrak, thinking that although it is foolish to praise oneself, prayer is the door to blessings.

You Named Manju

You, named Manju, reached the level of primordial accomplishment;
You, Sangyay Yeshe, attained the power of forceful mantra;
You, Dumgya Shangtrom, are the king of treasure revealers;
You, their miracle, Traktung Barway Dorje Tsal:
Nourish the good lotus garden of devoted disciples
With the sunlight of your blessing.

Written by Barway Dorje at the request of my disciple Rinchen.

Root of All Blessings and Siddhi

HUM! Root of all blessings and siddhi,
Essence of all victors of the three times,
True Vajradhara, kind lord guru:
I pray at the feet of Barway Dorje.
Dispel all obstacles to my three gates now and forever.
Bestow the holy blessings of the supreme and common siddhi.

No matter what thoughts suddenly arise in your mind—
Such as joy, sorrow, good, or bad—
Be natural in their freshness.
Do not alter whatever occurs, such as movement or stillness.
Continually sustain undistracted awareness.

Pray to your guru, yidam, and dakini
With belief, devotion, and fierce longing.
Saddened by samsara's endless work,
Yearn for liberation as the thirsty yearn for water.

At the request of the young mantrin Döndrup,
This was written by Dechen Barway Dorje
In the temple at the supreme place, Yudrak.
May dual benefit result. Virtue!

Complete Trikaya Teacher

NAMO GURU!
Complete trikaya teacher, Padmakara;
Manjushri, lord of body and knowledge;
Yamantaka, wrathful king who conquers Mara's forces;
All-seeing youthful guru heruka;
Great Splendor, Traktung Gaway Yeshe Tsal:
I pray to Dechen Barway Dorje.

Written by Barway Dorje at the request of Shenpen. Virtue!

This Fresh Mind

This fresh mind of ours is the actual buddha.
Sustaining unaltered awareness is prayer.
Unlimited appearances are the actual path.
The absence of doubt is all-sufficient conduct and fruition.

I pray to Barway Dorje, the embodiment of all buddhas,
With one-pointed faith and fierce devotion.
Hold me with compassion in this and all future lives and
between them.
Grant your blessing so that my continuum accords with
dharma.

Written by Barway Dorje at the request of Ani Könchok Zangmo. Virtue!

Blessed by Wisdom Devas and Dakinis

Blessed by wisdom devas and dakinis,
Great Splendor Traktung Gaway Yeshe,
Vidyadhara Dechen Barway Dorje,
Powerful Düdül Lingpa: I pray to you.

Written by Barway Dorje. May it bring virtue!

Bhaishajyaguru

Bhaishajyaguru who dispels the sickness of the five poisons,
And Barway Dorje who is indivisible from you:
I pray to you. Hold me with compassion.
Free me from sickness.

Written by Barway Dorje. May it bring virtue!

Great Splendor

Great Splendor, personification of all victors' compassion,
Traktung Dechen Barway Dorje Tsal,
Powerful Düdül Lingpa: I pray to you.
Grant your blessing so that adversity and obstacles are pacified,
So that my pure aspirations are accomplished in accord with dharma,
And so that I become indistinguishable from your body, speech, and mind.

Written by Barway Dorje at the request of the disciplinarian Karma Tapkay. Virtue!

Sun of Omniscience

NAMO GURU!
Sun of omniscience who dispels the darkness of ignorance,
Protector Manjushri, Lord of Speech, moon of brilliant knowledge;
And the Lion of Proclamation, Düdül Lingpa, indivisible from him:
I pray to you. Grant me brilliant intelligence.

Written by Barway Dorje for Jampal Rinchen Zangpo.

Guru Padmakara Who Embodies All the Three Roots

Guru Padmakara, who embodies all the three roots;
Compassionate guru, whose nature is the three jewels;
Shri Heruka Chokgyur Dechen Lingpa;
Great treasury of wisdom and love, guru, buddha, victor:
I pray to you with unbearably fierce devotion.

Guru Amitayus, who bestows actual immortality;
Guru God of Wealth, who increases prosperity;
Wish-fulfilling jewel, source of everything wanted:
I pray to you from my heart. Grant your blessing.
I pray that now and in the future, at all times,
You look upon me ceaselessly with compassion.

Glorious guru, may I possess a body like yours,
A retinue, a life span, a realm,
And a supreme name like yours.
May I become just like you.

Written by Barway Dorje at the request of the faithful Dorje Namgyal.

Vajradhara My Mind and Guru Indivisible

Vajradhara, my mind and guru indivisible:
I pray to Dechen Barway Dorje.
Grant your blessing that, unmoved by thoughts
And delusive appearances, I recognize my own true nature;
That I effortlessly perfect the four appearances
And naturally achieve the four vidyadhara levels;
And that I quickly attain the state of Samantabhadra.

Written by Barway Dorje at the request of Lama Puntsok. May it bring virtue!

Padma's Representative

Padma's representative, Tobden Düdül Lingpa,
Embodiment of all the three jewels, Vajradhara, Barway Dorje,
Scion of all victors, Samantabhadra of Uddiyana,
  indestructible vajra:
You uphold the victory banner of the teachings.
I pray to you and your lineage of father and sons.
May I employ my continuum in virtuous dharma.
May all present and future adversity and obstacles be pacified.
May my pure aspirations be accomplished according to my wishes.

Written by Barway Dorje at the request of many disciples, such as Kunga and Ani Chönyi Zangmo.

Vajradhara, Tilo, Naro

Vajradhara, Tilo, Naro,
Chökyi Lodrö, Shepa Dorje,
Dzamling Drakpa, glorious Düsum Khyenpa,
Jikten Sumgön, glorious Sherap Gyaltsen,
Karma Chakme, Barway Dorje,
And all root and lineage gurus who have promised
To transfer realization through blessing
To those who take the ultimate lineage as their root gurus:
I pray to you.

Self-illuminating self-awareness is without meditation.
May I sustain mere undistracted mindfulness
Unpolluted by excitement, depression, or the undercurrent.
May I not get lost in mindless bewilderment.
May I ceaselessly recollect impermanence, death, and devotion.
May I remain without hope, fear, removal, or accomplishment,
In the all-pervasive expanse of unaltered, ordinary cognition.
May I become indistinguishable from the mind of my very kind guru.

Written by Barway Dorje at the request of Lodrö Zangmo. Virtue!

You Protect from All Danger

NAMO GURU!
You protect us from all danger
And cause the accomplishment of our wishes according to dharma.
Three roots; three jewels;
Bhaishajyaguru; Avalokita;
Mother Tara, who protects from the eight dangers;
Yamantaka, who turns away enemies and demons;
Marichi, who protects from robbery;
Shavari, who dispels sickness;
Jambhala, who dispels poverty;
Padmakara, who embodies all the three roots;
And my root guru, all of these indivisible:
I pray to you with unreserved longing.

In bad, decadent times all sentient beings
Display their degeneracy through restlessness.
Unable to stay in one place,
We seek hidden lands.
I pray that you guide us on our way.
Grant your blessing that we be without obstacles.

So that we are safe on rivers, in boats, and on bridges;
And so that we are safe from predators and robbers,
I ask you—mother, protector, Vajrasadhu,
Twelve Tenmas, Tseringma, those with samaya,
Treasure-lords, and site-lords—
To guide us on our way to hidden places.

Wherever we go and wherever we stay,
May our lives be long and without sickness.
May experiences, realization, food, clothing,
Grain, wealth, and affluence increase.
Cause our wishes to be fulfilled.

Written by Dechen Barway Dorje on a good day in the Sun Moon Cave of Kyijam at the request of a tutor from Thrangu Monastery. May it bring virtue!

A Prayer and Aspiration for Protection from Pain at Death

OM AH HUM NAMO GURU DHARMAKAYA BODHISATTVAYE!
Bodhisattva Dispeller of All Obscurations,
As you vowed in the past,
Free us from adversity at death.
Pacify pain and suffering at death.

Akashagarbha, dispel the darkness of our minds.
Heroic Manjushri, bestow the illumination of prajna.
Samantabhadra, introduce the mother and son clear lights.
Lord Maitreya, kindly protect us from the suffering of downfall.
Avalokita, lead us away from bad migrations.
Kshitigarbha, protect us from the suffering of hunger and thirst.
Vajrapani, I pray that you protect us from the menace
Of gandharvas, slayers, yamas, and elementals.

Guru, may we recognize the dharmakaya's clear light.
May we be liberated in the natural interval of the sambhogakaya.
May we not be fettered by the appearances of nirmanakaya's migration.
May we gain confidence in the innate perfection of the trikaya.
May we see through dreamlike, illusory birth and death.
May the suffering of death be quickly dispelled.

The pain of the elements is like the water of a mirage.
May the deluded mind, like a deer, not seek to drink it.
In the state of recognizing its nature,
May self-awareness, Samantabhadra, be instantly revealed.

OM AH HUM HRIH OM MANI PADME HUM DHARE DHARE BHANDHARE SVAHA

Recite this as many times as possible. Written quickly by Dechen Barway Dorje at the request of my disciple Lodrö Chödrak.

The Guru's Body is Manjushri

NAMO GURU!
The guru's body is Manjushri,
The Lion of Proclamation, who dispels darkness.
I pray to you. Bless me.
Dispel my obscuration by dullness and ignorance.

The guru's speech is Avalokita,
The Compassionate One, who dispels attachment.
I pray to you. Bless me.
Pacify my delusion and craving.

The guru's mind is Vajrapani,
The Lord of Secrets, who dispels anger.
I pray to you. Bless me.
Pacify agitation and madness.

Whatever arises in self-awareness is the guru's mind.
May I sustain its nature without alteration.

All that appears or exists is the guru's body.
By meditating on pure appearances may I tame my mind.

Whatever I hear—good or bad—is the victors' speech.
May I view it all as the sound of mantra.

May obstacles to my three gates be pacified.
May I finally attain buddhahood.

Written by Barway Dorje at the request of Karma Loden Palzang. May it bring virtue!

Lord of Boundless Light and Life

Lord of Boundless Light and Life; Avalokita; Padmakara,
Tamer of beings, our only protector in this time of degeneracy;
And my root guru, indivisible from them:
I pray to you with devotion and fierce longing.
Pacify sicknesses, demons, and obstacles of my three gates.
Grant your blessing so that I will always accord with dharma.

Samsara is like a river of suffering.
Birth, aging, sickness, and death are like bubbles and dreams.
Seeing that nothing is permanent or stable,
May I never mistake any composite to be real.

Hated enemies and beloved companions are uncertain.
One can become the other.
If we fixate on them as permanent, we are not free.
The momentum of actions is unstoppable, like waves in water.
Therefore, search for contentment within your continuum.

Prayer to the guru brings lasting benefit both present and future.
Devotion from your heart brings blessings.
Practice recitation, chanting, prostrations, and
  circumambulation.
Sustain fresh, continuous, undistracted awareness in your mind.
Without doubt, hope, or fear, sustain mere attention
Free from distraction or meditation.
Inspire your continuum with compassion,
Knowing all beings to be your parents;
And impermanence, knowing that you will soon die.
Be vigorous in dharma, knowing that there is no time to spare.

Written quickly by old Barway Dorje as an aspiration to dispel the sadness of Dayang, a woman dear to my heart. May all her wishes be fulfilled in accord with dharma!

Great Splendor Supreme Heruka

OM MAHA SHRI HERUKA NAMAYE!
Great Splendor, Supreme Heruka;
Perfect King, ruler of the matrikas of samsara and nirvana;
And Powerful Black One, slayer who conquers the vicious:
I pray to you. Bestow the siddhi of might and power.

Tamer of All the Haughty, enemy of maras and slayer of elementals;
Vajrakumara, conqueror of the four maras;
And Great Splendor Hayagriva, slayer of the five poisons and elementals:
I pray to you. Bestow the siddhi of might and power.

Outshiner of Seals, king of all samsara and nirvana;
Padmakara, who outshines all who appear and exist;
And Dorje Tritsun, whose might is unstoppable:
I pray to you. Bestow the siddhi of might and power.

A vajravidyadhara indistinguishable from the deities,
You possess the celestial wisdom of great bliss.
Barway Dorje, you outshine all incorrect thoughts.
I pray to you. Bestow the siddhi of might and power.

Through the splendid blessing of the ferocious Powerful Black One
And the activity of Padma, master of all who appear or exist,
You consume in space the hearts' blood of obstructors and elementals.
I pray to the supremely glorious heruka.

The glorious protectors, those with samaya in the places and realms,
And the world's guardians await your commands.

You place negative elementals under samaya.
I pray to the great hero who subdues the haughty.

The Victor's teaching you treasure as your own heart.
The Victor's teaching's essence, secret mantra, you spread in the ten directions.
The victors' lord Padma's activity you expand to the limits of space.
The victors' son, Chökyi Senge: I pray to you.

Through the power of this prayer to the holy,
May the damaged elements of the external environment be restored.
May excellence and virtue blaze with splendor.
May fruit, crops, and livestock always flourish.

May beings' internal darkness be eradicated.
May sickness, famine, warfare, and obstacles be pacified.
May beings possess longevity, affluence, and the fulfillment of their wants and wishes.
May the teachings and beings prosper without impairment.

In summary, may our intentions accord with dharma.
May obstacles to the levels and paths be pacified.
May experience and realization wax like the moon.
May we become indistinguishable from the guru
In our spontaneous accomplishment of dual benefit.

As well, may vicious, haughty spirits and rakshasas
Never stray from the victors' commands,
The vidyadharas' orders, and the holy gurus' samaya.
May they quickly accomplish conquest and care.
GURU VAJRA SARVA SAMAYA KA VA CHI RAKSHA HUM

This prayer and invocation accord with the present place, time, and circumstances. There have appeared signs that its regular recitation by those with devotion will cause virtue immediately and throughout the future. This was dictated by Dechen Barway Dorje to my disciple Karma Dulwa Lhadar in the dharma encampment of Tashika near Bhachen Yikgyal, the highest of the eighteen hills in the hidden valley of Nyeshung. May all who read, learn, or even keep a copy of this receive the blessings of the gurus of the three lineages, be victorious over obstacles and adversity, and be able to outshine and employ the haughty and all elementals. SARVA SUJAYA!

Indivisible from My Kind Root Guru

Om ah hum!
Indivisible from my kind root guru,
Sugata bhagavat Bhaishajyaguru;
Luwang Gyalpo; the thousand and two buddhas;
Arya Tara; Shavari;
Queen of Medicine, who dispels sickness;
And all who pacify sickness and demons: I pray to you.
I pray that you quickly pacify and protect me from
All sicknesses caused by karma or demons.

Wrathful Guru's emanations as a pig, scorpion, and garuda;
The great garudas of the five families who subdue elementals and slay time-demons;
And the red and black Hayagrivakilas, the deities who subdue the haughty:
I pray to you with one-pointed devotion and longing.
Do not forget your intentions and promises!
I pray that you turn away through the force of your intentions
All delusion and sickness caused by karma and demons.
I pray that you turn away all sicknesses caused by disturbed elements,
All epidemics caused by the breath of agitated spirits or by matrikas,
And all contagious diseases.

Through the power of this prayer to the sources of refuge,
May we enjoy glorious health of body and mind.
May the qualities of the ten virtuous actions steadily increase.

OM VAKISHVARI MUM
OM MANI PADME HUM
OM VAJRAPANI HUM
OM PADMA SHAVARI NEN PAR SHIK NAGA NEN SVAHA

Recite that aloud. Written by Barway Dorje at the request of Tengyay, Tentra, Sötön, and Zöpa. May it bring virtue!

Notes

1. Shepa Dorje was the name given Jetsun Milarepa by the deities of the Chakrasamvara mandala. Barway Dorje, whose many names included Karma Jikme Chökyi Senge Trinlay Kunkyap (Karma Fearless Dharma Lion Pervasive Activity) and Pal Traktung Gaway Yeshe Dechen Barway Dorje Tobden Dudul Lingpa (Glorious Heruka Joyous Wisdom Great Bliss Blazing Vajra Powerful Tamer of Maras), was an emanation of Milarepa. Guru Rinpoche is often called Uddiyana because he once ruled that land.

2. The five excellent vidyadharas were five beings, not all of them human, who received Vajrayana teaching from the bodhisattva Vajrapani soon after the Buddha's parinirvana.

3. The first part of this song is also found in Barway Dorje's autobiography.

4. The five kinds of beings ("baby birds") are those of the six types, with the asuras included in the deva realm and not listed separately.

5. The eight qualities of mastery are subtle form, visible form, lightness, all-pervasiveness, perfect attainment, utter clarity, stability, and the acquisition of all that is desired.

6. Fivefold degeneration refers to the degeneration of behavior, kleshas, views, life span, and nutrition.
7. Yishin means "according to your wishes;" Norbu is "jewel." This is a play on the name of the teacher to whom the song was addressed.
8. The four impossibilities are the child of a childless woman, the horns of a rabbit, the hair of a tortoise, and a flower growing in the sky. Since it was believed that elephants lack saliva, the saliva of elephants could be considered one as well.
9. Jikme Chökyi Senge, one of Barway Dorje's names.
10. A six-legged warrior is a bee. His feast is honey, which represents fine speech.
11. The six-syllable and hundred-syllable mantras are those of Vajrasattva.
12. Kirtidhvaja is Drakpa Gyaltsen; Mati and Punya are Lodrö Rinchen and Sönam Zangpo respectively.
13. The duration of the Buddha's teaching is divided into five-hundred year periods, each more degenerate than the previous one.
14. The sixteen pure human dharmas were originally sixteen commands of the dharma king Songtsen Gampo. They are: 1. The veneration of the three jewels; 2. The study and practice of the holy dharma; 3. The repayment of one's parents' kindness; 4. Respect for the learned; 5. Service of the noble and the aged; 6. Assisting one's neighbors; 7. Truthfulness and modesty; 8. Patience within the family; 9. Emulation of those with probity; 10. Moderation in food and wealth; 11. Loyalty to previous benefactors; 12. The timely repayment of debts and honesty in business; 13. Having little jealousy of anyone; 14. Independence and discretion regarding bad advice; 15. Gentle and moderate speech; and 16. Altruistic open-mindedness.
15. All-Seeing is an epithet of Manjushri, whose wrathful form, Yamantaka, is sometimes called Outshines All Seals. Barway Dorje was an emanation of Manjushri, and Stable Wheel is yet another name for Manjushri.

16. SARVA SUJAYA means "Full victory for all."

17. Mipam Trinlay Kunkyap is another of Barway Dorje's names.

18. The italicized words are Barway Dorje's full name.

19. Arising-liberation occurs when the arising of a thought is accompanied by liberating awareness.

20. The Great Repa is Milarepa.

21. Vajradhara, here referred to as Mahavajradhara, is called the sixth buddha because he embodies all five buddha families.

22. The three concerns are eating, sleeping, and eliminating.

23. Kagyü Tashi was the editor of this book. The introductory paragraph and those colophons to the individual songs that refer to Barway Dorje in the third person were written by Kagyü Tashi unless otherwise specified. Many of the colophons, however, were written by Barway Dorje himself. In available editions of this book in Tibetan, there is no final colophon to the text as a whole; the book ends with the colophon to the last song.

24. The authorized seals are the points of view and conduct that distinguish an authentic follower of the Buddha.

25. The four feet of miracle are the qualities achieved on the greater path of accumulation.

26. The dakinis' reception is a sign of possible impending death for a realized yogin.

27. Yunying Özer was named after Yudra Nyingpo, a great disciple of the Dzokchen master Vairochana. Leapover is one of the two main aspects of Dzokchen practice.

28. Triple isolation is isolation of body, speech, and mind. Summer's drum is thunder.

29. The two traditions are secular and spiritual virtue.

30. Fourfold faith includes belief, awe, aspiration, and irreversability.

31. Fourfold generosity is the giving of material things, protection, dharma, and love.

32. The four limits are existence, nonexistence, both, and neither.

33. Mahamudra means "Great Seal."

34. Lerap Düdjom Dorje was the name of the incarnation of Kyodrak Dungtrul Rinpoche who lived concurrently with Barway Dorje.

35. Words quoted here from "The Spontaneous Vajra Song of Awareness-Emptiness" are in italic.

36. These are liberation through seeing, hearing, recollecting, wearing, touching, or tasting.

37. There are two types of pratyekabuddhas. Rhinolike pratyekabuddhas live alone; parrotlike pratyekabuddhas live in communities.

List of Songs

Acknowledgments

We would like to gratefully thank Bardor Tulku Rinpoche for his inspiration; Lama Tashi Tobgyal for providing the Tibetan text and kindly answering our questions; and Jigme Nyima and Florence Wetzel for their editorial assistance.

Yeshe Gyamtso, Maureen McNicholas,
and Peter van Deurzen

The Third Barway Dorje Tulku Rinpoche.

Kunzang Palchen Ling

The Third Barway Dorje Tulku Rinpoche, Karma Drupgyü Tenpay Nyima, teaches the treasures of Terchen Barway Dorje at Kunzang Palchen Ling, All-Good Great Splendor Park, in Red Hook, New York. Those interested in finding out more about Rinpoche's teachings and activities, or in supporting Raktrul Monastery in Eastern Tibet, may contact:

Kunzang Palchen Ling
Red Hook, New York
www.Kunzang.org

Karma Triyana Dharmachakra

Karma Triyana Dharmachakra (KTD) is the North American seat of His Holiness the Gyalwang Karmapa, and under the spiritual guidance and protection of His Holiness Ogyen Trinley Dorje, the Seventeenth Gyalwang Karmapa, is devoted to the authentic representation of the Kagyu lineage of Tibetan Buddhism.

For information regarding KTD, including our current schedule, or for information regarding our affiliate centers, Karma Thegsum Choling (KTC), located both in the United States and internationally, contact us using the information below.

Karma Triyana Dharmachakra
335 Meads Mountain Road
Woodstock, NY, 12498 USA
845 679 5906 ext. 10
www.kagyu.org
KTC Coordinator: 845 679 5701
ktc@kagyu.org

KTD Publications

Gathering the garlands of the gurus' precious teachings

KTD Publications, a part of Karma Triyana Dharmachakra, is a not-for-profit publisher established with the purpose of facilitating the projects and activities manifesting from His Holiness's inspiration and blessings. We are dedicated to gathering the garlands of precious teachings and producing fine-quality books.

We invite you to join KTD Publications in facilitating the activities of His Holiness Karmapa and fulfilling the wishes of Khenpo Karthar Rinpoche and Bardor Tulku Rinpoche. If you would like to sponsor a book or make a donation to KTD Publications, please contact us using the information below. All contributions are tax-deductible.

KTD Publications
335 Meads Mountain Road
Woodstock, NY, 12498 USA
Telephone: 845 679 5906 ext. 37
www.KTDPublications.org

Also from www.KTD Publications.org

Karma Chakme's Mountain Dharma as Taught by Khenpo Karthar Rinpoche, Volume One, translated by Yeshe Gyamtso and Chojor Radha, 2005; *Volume Two*, translated by Yeshe Gyamtso, 2006; *Volume Three*, translated by Yeshe Gyamtso and Chojor Radha, 2007; *Volumes Four and Five*, 2008

Precious Essence: The Inner Autobiography of Terchen Barway Dorje, translated by Yeshe Gyamtso, 2005

The Vajra Garland & The Lotus Garden: Treasure Biographies of Padmakara and Vairochana, translated by Yeshe Gyamtso, 2005

Nyima Tashi: The Songs and Instructions of the First Traleg Kyabgön Rinpoche, translated by Yeshe Gyamtso, English and Tibetan, 2006

Chariot of the Fortunate: The Life of the First Yongey Mingyur Dorje by Je Tukyi Dorje & Surmang Tendzin Rinpoche, translated by Yeshe Gyamtso, English and Tibetan, 2006

Bardo: Interval of Possibility, Khenpo Karthar Rinpoche, translated by Yeshe Gyamtso, 2006

A Ceremony of Offering to the Gurus, the 17th Gyalwang Karmapa, Ogyen Trinley Dorje, translated by Yeshe Gyamtso; India, 2006; USA, 2007

The Dalai Lama in Woodstock: Celebrating the United Nations International Day of Peace, Full color photo book, 2007

Garland of Jewels: The Eight Bodhisattvas, by Ju Mipham Rinpoche, translated by Yeshe Gyamtso, 2007

The Kagyu Monlam Book, the 17th Gyalwang Karmapa, Ogyen Trinley Dorje, 2007

Karma Chakme's Very Concise Union of Mahamudra and Dzokchen, Khenpo Karthar Rinpoche, translated by Yeshe Gyamtso, 2007

May all beings be happy.